MARYANN KASPER

THE
ART
OF
BELIEVING

"CLAIMING GOD'S PROMISES FOR A
LIFE OF PEACE, POWER, AND PURPOSE."

The Art of Believing
Copyright © 2024 by MaryAnn Kasper

This book is self-published in collaboration with: Rainy Day Self-Publishing LLC
RainyDaySelfPublishing.com

Unless otherwise marked, all scripture quotations are from *The Holy Bible*, New International Version®, NIV® Copyright © 1973, 1978, 1984, 2011 by Biblica, Inc.® Used by permission. All rights reserved worldwide.

Scripture quotations marked (ESV) are from *The ESV® Bible (The Holy Bible, English Standard Version®)*. ESV® Text Edition: 2016. Copyright © 2001 by Crossway, a publishing ministry of Good News Publishers. The ESV® text has been reproduced in cooperation with and by permission of Good News Publishers. Unauthorized reproduction of this publication is prohibited. All rights reserved.

Scripture quotations marked (MSG) are from *The Message Bible*, copyright © 1993, 2002, 2018 by Eugene H. Peterson. Used by permission of NavPress. All rights reserved. Represented by Tyndale House Publishers, Inc.

Scripture quotations marked (NLT) are from the *Holy Bible*, New Living Translation, copyright © 1996, 2004, 2015 by Tyndale House Foundation. Used by permission of Tyndale House Publishers, Inc., Carol Stream, Illinois 60188. All rights reserved.

Scripture quotations marked (NKJV) are from the New King James Version®. Copyright © 1982 by Thomas Nelson. Used by permission. All rights reserved.

Coloring Pages & Artwork: MaryAnn Kasper on Canva.

Canva designs are used within their legal commercial license, stated within their agreement, seen here: "Content licenses and using Canva for commercial purposes." Canva, https://www.canva.com/help/article/licenses-copyright-legal-commercial-use/.

Cover Design: Ella @ Book Company and MaryAnn Kasper

The specialty font in this document is 100% free for commercial use. It belongs to its original creator! For more information, see:
Twinkle Star: https://fonts.google.com/specimen/Twinkle+Star

First Publication: April 2024

For additional copies or bulk purchases, visit:
http://amazon.com/author/maryannkasper

KDP ISBN: 979-8-9865174-0-7
B&N Press ISBN: 979-8-9865174-1-4

Dedication

To the Faithful in the Lord,
The One Who Made the Promises is Faithful.

Acknowledgements

I am grateful for Barb and the rest of the North Jersey Christian Writer's Group who encouraged me each month to keep going in my writing, Karla's Actors & Writers Group who gave me input and helped me make progress with our three-hour weekly sessions, and the Breakfast Club ladies who loved me through the years even when I acted unlovable (and later gave me valuable feedback on my manuscript). To Gloria, my spiritual coach, who kept me believing even when I doubted. To Joey, my best friend and husband, for his constant love and support, and to our three sons, Zach, Harry, and Hunter who inspire me every day with their courage, talents, and abilities. *Commit yourselves to the Lord and follow your dreams in Him.*

Contents

Introduction

Trouble

"I have told you these things so that you may have peace in me. In this world you will have trouble. But take heart! I have overcome the world."

John 16:33

I woke up this morning, head pounding, still feeling anxious and dismayed from the previous day's work. *I need my headache medicine*, I thought and realized this has been going on for too long.

My husband said, "Maybe you should look for another job. It can't hurt to look."

Lately, it's been happening almost every weekend. For some unknown reason, I can get through my stressful school week, headache-free, only for it to hit me all at once when I've let down my guard come Saturday morning.

Now I'm beginning to wonder, *is my body telling me something? Do I want to be a teacher? But I just got tenure AND completed my master's degree last spring. If I stay, I'll get a raise next school year.* What should I do?

My teaching assignment has been emotionally challenging this year (as it was last year and the year before). I've had my share of conflicts with students, parents, teaching staff, and administration, but I've worked things through and feel I'm making a difference in my school community. I'm learning new teaching strategies and growing spiritually, as well.

Does it have to be this hard? What if I go to another district and I feel the same way? And I really don't want to go through the hassle of updating my resume and writing those terrible cover letters. What is God's will in this matter? How do I know I'm making the right decision? Lord, help me. Guide me to the path that's right for me.

As I sit on the couch in my struggle, many emotions wash over me: sadness, worry, and hopelessness, and then it happens just as it's happened for the last 27 years since I first became a follower of Christ. A scripture came to mind shining a light on my situation, "What are mere mortals that you should think about them, human beings that you should care for them? Yet you made them only a little lower than God and crowned them with glory and honor. You gave them charge of everything you made, putting everything under their authority - the flocks and the herds and all the wild animals, the birds in the sky, the fish in the sea, and everything that swims the ocean currents."[1]

He cares about me. I am one of His honorable creations, I reasoned with myself.

Although He's the authority over my life, He's put me in charge of the choices that I make regarding my life such as whether I should stay or leave my current position. And I trust He will help guide me to the right kind of work because it's for my good and His glory that He does.

Moments later, I emerge with newfound hope. That's the power of the Word of God. It changed my attitude from hopeless to hopeful with just one verse.

Yes, God cares for me and sees me in my dilemma. He reminds me He is working for my good and His glory.[2]

Believing His Word and trusting that He is guiding me will require faith and effort on my part. I will need to check the Sunday paper each week and apply to ads that look like a good fit. I will need to write a cover letter and update my resume. But God promises He will be with me through it all.

The Art of Believing is about living faithfully with action and holding onto the promises He offers us. We must do the work He calls us to do because we know He has the best plans and is leading us in the direction we are to go.

Help in Our Weakness

I write this book in weakness. And oh, how liberating it is to do so. Why? Because it is here where I rely on God's strength. It is here where I am humble, and remember I am flesh and blood. This is where Jesus meets me and gently reminds me, He's got my back. He knows my anxious thoughts and makes a way in the desert leading me through uncharted waters and chaotic situations. It's in the unknown where His power works in ways I cannot always see or fathom.

When I don't know which road to take, I remember His Words. "Your ears will hear Him. Right behind you, a voice will say, 'This is the way you should go,' whether to the right or the left,"[3] and, "He guides me to every right path."[4]

I trust He's preparing something good for me because He says, "(I am His) handiwork, created in Christ Jesus to do good works, which God prepared in advance for (me) to do."[5]

This is just one of the many promises we can be confident in with Jesus.

I hope that by reading this book, you will live your days peacefully while relying on God's power as you hold onto His promises. Together we will learn to submit to and go after His perfect plans for our lives. But be warned. His plans may look different than ours. Still, be glad because His ways are higher than ours, and we can trust that His plans are the best.[6]

As we journey through our lives with God, there may be different twists and turns throughout our seasons together. Sometimes the doors of opportunity will open with minimal effort. There will be laughter and light-heartedness, peace, and trust. At other times it might seem all the doors have closed shut. You might find yourself in a difficult situation. There will be trouble, tears, and doubts. There may be obstacles to overcome. But we don't lose hope or revert to our old patterns. Instead, we stay faithful and ride out the storms. We continue to trust, pray, and read our Bibles. We get with spiritual friends to help us along the way who will pray for us. But we plan and take one day at a time to reach our goal to live faithfully with Him until the end.

"For I know the plans I have for you, declares the Lord, plans to prosper you and not harm you, plans to give you hope and a future."[7]

Let's journey together and live more peaceful and powerful lives as we trust God to fulfill His promises with the plans He has for each one of us.

Questions

1. Read 2 Corinthians 12:1-10 (NLT). In verses 9(b)-10, Paul says, "So now I am glad to boast about my weaknesses, so that the power of Christ can work through me." Whose power is Paul relying on in his weakness? Whose power should we be relying on?

_____

_____

_____

2. Consider the following verses: Psalm 18:30, "As for God, His ways are perfect," and Genesis 1:27, "So God created man in His image." Do you think He expects our ways to be perfect like His? Write down what this means to you.

_____

_____

_____

_____

3. As a Christian, do you have difficulty accepting that you need a Savior? Do you often try to hide your weaknesses, or find it difficult to admit you've made a mistake? Do you have a hard time believing God loves you and accepts you because you put your trust in what Jesus did on the cross, not because of what you did or didn't do? If so, reflect and journal about this before moving on to the next chapter. (Read Rom 3:22 for help understanding this).

_____

_____

_____

_____

Reflection

I struggled with anxiety at work and with my relationships there and wanted to leave my job. I did the following things as I prayed to surrender to God's will for me.

First, I bought the Sunday paper and looked through the want ads. After searching for three weeks and finding nothing, I became grateful for my current job. But I still needed to convince myself I should stay.

Next, I looked online and found a position at an alternative school. The requirements needed were a perfect fit for me. I sent them my resume and received a phone interview the same week. When I first spoke with the recruiter, I was enthusiastic, but after driving by to see the school in person,

I began to have doubts. Thankfully, they never called me back.

Then, I met my friends for breakfast and told them about my dilemma with my co-workers. One friend had a similar situation at her work, but instead of quitting, she started praying for them. The next time she went to her office, her colleague's attitude softened toward her, and she even gave my friend a spiritual book. Now they are friends, and her workplace is a more peaceful place.

I began praying for my relationships at work.

The next day, I looked for ways I could encourage my co-workers. Two opportunities came my way; one co-worker was selling cookies for her son's fundraiser, and I purchased some. Another co-worker needed copying, and I offered to do it for her. To date, both relationships have improved because of these simple acts. Prayer with action is powerful!

After more input and reflection, leaving my job became less of an urgent need. I realized much of my anxiety came from the 30-minute lunch duty gig I took on for extra money. This harmless half-hour added so much stress to my already challenging day that I decided to finish out the year but not sign up for it again. It wasn't worth it.

In conclusion, I felt led to stay in my current position. I am beyond grateful for this realization and at peace with the outcome. Now I was confident this is where He wanted me to be. When the new contract came into my mailbox for the next school year, I happily signed it with newfound hope for what would come.

Here's what I learned: God allowed me to struggle with my relationships at work so I could imitate Jesus and practice loving two difficult co-workers. He gave me gratitude for my job and confidence that this is where I should stay. In addition, He gave me the wisdom to turn down extra money to have peace of mind. I would never have come to these conclusions unless I had prayed, believed, acted, and received, with gratitude.

What situation, relationship, or another dilemma. big or small, have you been struggling with this week, month, or year?

_____

_____

_____

_____

Use the acronym P.A.R.T. to "part with" or give God your worries about your struggle.

- **Pray**: Tell God about your struggle/request. He is listening and working on your behalf!
- **Act**: Wait, listen, watch, read scripture, or get with a trusted spiritual friend who can give you feedback on what to do next. Decide what you'll do and do it.
- **Receive**: Accept where you are regarding your struggle. Trust God is working in this waiting period, or He may be maturing you for greater things to come.
- **Thank God**: Pray again thanking God for working on your behalf.

Write down ideas that come to mind such as to whom you will get advice, what scriptures will be helpful, and what decisions you will make.

_____

_____

_____

_____

God's Promise

"Do not be anxious about anything, but in every situation, by prayer and petition, with thanksgiving, present your requests to God. And the peace of God which transcends all understanding, will guard your hearts and minds in Christ Jesus."

With a thankful heart, write down any requests you have for God in the space below.

_____

_____

_____

_____

Write down your top 5 areas of life where your faith is small and worry/anxiety tends to take over. Then in the box to the right, rate them on a scale of 1-10.* As you color the memory verse below, give your anxieties to Jesus and ask Him to work with you in each of these areas.

Cast all your anxiety on him because he cares for you.
1 Peter 5:7 (b)

*10 means I'm not worried at all, you're faithful God is working and 1 is extremely worried/you lack faith, God is not working in this area of my life.

Believe

Part 1

Believe

The purposes for writing this book were two-fold: First, I wanted to walk with God in such a way as to claim the promises of peace in the Bible He was offering me. My life was filled with so much anxiety that I knew there had to be a better way.

However, when I searched the scriptures and prayed, the events in my life seemed to grow even more challenging. I had to dig deeper into my faith than ever before. What I did in the past was no longer working, the need for people's approval, my pride, and deceitfulness. It was time to let them go.

Second, I was determined to live a powerful life. I wanted to live out the plans He had in store for me even though I knew this would require humility, surrender, and trust on my part. But Jesus said He would be with me.

Jesus is the One who went before me and is always with me, my Advocate through life's ups and downs. The One I can trust who has overcome suffering and given me the pardon to live fully without shame or regret. Since He thought I was worth dying for, made plans for my life, and offered me so many promises, shouldn't I make it my goal to follow through with my end of the deal?

How about you?

Thought Questions

1. Why can we put our trust in God?

2. How do trials strengthen our faith?

3. What does trust have to do with surrender?

Chapter One

Trusting God

"Trust in the Lord with all your heart and lean not on your own understanding; in all your ways submit to him and he will make your paths straight."

Proverbs 3:5-6

In complete surrender, I prayed the following prayer in June of last school year, not knowing what grade or subjects I'd teach in the fall.

Lord, although you have blessed me beyond words, I ask that you place me in the position I will enjoy that fits my strengths and weaknesses and satisfies my inner need to help others see their giftedness and help them along their journey in life. Give me an encouraging work environment that is peaceful and supportive and pays at least what I'm making now, plus the increase I'm supposed to get because I earned my master's degree this year. Oh, and while you're at it, please give me a room with a desk since I didn't get one last year. I'll even be glad to share it with others if needed. Amen.

Why is it so challenging to surrender our plans to God? Why is it so difficult for us to believe God wants to give us good gifts? The best gifts? I could tell you about my upbringing that made me doubt this. I'm sure many of us could. Because of the way we may have been treated in the past, we have difficulty believing God loves us. We must understand and work through where these falsehoods come from and be careful not to let them interfere with our relationship with God.

Inner Child Healing

A friend of mine told me about an audio meditation that helped her overcome the bad feelings she harbored in her heart as an adult when she was left to care for her younger siblings. She was only a child herself when her parents' needed money and had to go to work leaving her with their childcare responsibility. She felt she never had a childhood of her own.

She began the healing process by listening to an *Inner Child Healing Meditation by Joanne.*[1] This meditation taught her how to nurture the wounded parts of the little girl inside of her who she said, "still gets frightened," at times. Regularly listening to the meditation helped her to heal her wounded parts and allowed her to trust and receive God's love as a grown woman today.

Revisiting the Past

Sometimes our old belief patterns prevent us from believing who we are in Christ and claiming the promises He offers us. In these cases, it might be helpful to revisit the past so we can move past those areas in which we're stuck.

Even in situations where it was our own wrongdoing, we can still find truth and grace when we come to God with a humble, contrite, and repentant heart. He is a merciful and forgiving God.

Revisiting the past with a trusted friend or counselor can be helpful in that it can shed light on a matter and expose what was the truth. We can then see clearly to begin to rewrite the script in our hearts and minds and bring about healing.

Working through our pasts may be difficult, but as we heal, we will not only be better able to receive God's love, mercy, forgiveness and promises but also be able to give it freely to others.

Deepening Our Trust in God

"Trust in the Lord with all your heart and lean not on your own understanding. In all your ways acknowledge Him, and He will make your paths straight." [2]

As I read these words at bedtime to my then-four-year-old son, Zach, I rolled his small Matchbox® car across his night table in a straight path. I would then re-read the scripture again in its opposite form. "But if you *don't* trust the Lord with all of your heart and you lean on your *own* understanding," I continued, "And if you *don't* acknowledge Him in all of your ways, then...*CRASH!*" and I would slide the car across the table, fast and furious, so it crashed and fell to the floor.

He loved this activity. Night after night, he would ask me to do it again and again.

But you know what? It stuck with him.

When he turned eighteen, he decided to study the Bible with several members of his teen ministry at church. He became a Christian in 2017. My husband and I can't take much credit for his decision. We tried our best to live faithfully. But we made plenty of mistakes.

The things we may have gotten right; we read our Bibles regularly, we prayed, we took him with us to church services, and our closest friendships were with families in the church whose kids were in the same age group. We participated in youth and family activities and taught in the children's classes. We even helped at the teen camps in the summer.

These activities may have aided Zach becoming a Christian, but it was God who beckoned him. In his own words, he stated, "The way I was living my life and the trouble I almost got into was enough to realize my way wasn't working." So, when the timing was right, he knew where to go to study the Bible.

We must learn to trust God's timing for all good things because even when it feels as if nothing is happening, He is still working.

Love Songs

In writing this book, my heart's desire was to learn to trust God so I could believe and receive all He had to offer me, the promises of peace, of His power, and love. I wanted it all. I knew once I was able to receive these things, I might then have the capacity to give them back to others, without expecting anything in return.

But I had to learn a few things.

Primarily, I had to believe God at His Word and act as if I believed it. But first, I needed to understand how deeply He loved me.

Did you ever watch a love story where two actors stared into the eyes of each other and spoke words of tenderness, desire, and truth to one another? Okay, they were just acting but wouldn't you want it if it really existed?

Due to past rejection, some of us may not think this kind of trust and intimacy with someone can really exist, or if it does, it's short lived. Even Jesus didn't put His trust in people because He knew what was in a man.

But I dare to say that we can absolutely put our trust in God and have an intimate relationship with Him because of His perfection and because of who He says we are in Him.

One day while on my normal morning jog, I listened to a song called The Best[3] by Tina Turner. When I read the lyrics later on, I decided it must be about two people who had a deep and vulnerable relationship with one another. This lover met her every need, kept his promises, and fulfilled her dreams. She came to him with her rawest emotions, and he reassured her of his love. They sounded like they were on a wild, passionate adventure together, completely in love.

Although the humans in this love relationship will fail each other at one time or another, I liken this song to my relationship with Jesus and the wildly in love ride of life we are on together. Passionate. Trusting. Adventurous. Steady.

Just as Jesus trusted His Father completely with the plans for His life, I can too.

I can trust God this way because of what the scriptures say about His character. I trust He loves me because He let His son suffer and die for me to pardon my sins and save me from condemnation. I believe He has the best plan for my life because He formed me in my mother's womb and equipped me for every good work He will have me do.

I encourage you to listen to this song or find one of your own. Sing the song from your heart to Him and imagine Him singing it back to you. Let it stir up the passion in your heart as you put your trust in Jesus. Then see if it will spark a deeper intimacy in your relationship with God.

Safe Relationships

I belong to a healthy family group in my church. Because we meet regularly, I have seen people grow in their faith, heal old wounds, and learn to experience joy in the vocations to which God has called them.

I've been open and vulnerable with my brothers and sisters within this group. Sometimes this meant I'd share my work, home, or family struggles with them. Other times I'd bring up misunderstandings.

Resolving conflicts with one another can be challenging and scary to do. But what I find helpful is to pray beforehand, be humble, and use "I" statements.

When we use "I" statements instead of "You" statements, it usually takes people off the defensive and enables the person to hear you out. For example, say "I felt hurt when you told my family I forgot to pick up the drycleaning," instead of accusing someone outright, "You put me down in front of my family."

It may feel uncomfortable to share your feelings with someone in the moment. But if trust and intimacy is to develop, share you must. Look at it as if you are giving someone the gift of your heart with the hope that your relationship will grow stronger because of it.

In the same way, we may be angry at God for a while because He doesn't give us something we want. Or someone else gets something we've worked hard to attain. But after a time, we return to Him and confess our bad feelings. He in return, comforts, encourages, and guides us along the pathway that belongs to us.

Who We Are in Christ

In Ephesians 2:8-9, Paul says, "God saved you by His special favor when you believed. And you can't take credit for this: It is a gift from God. Salvation is not a reward for our good deeds, so no one can boast about it, for we are God's masterpieces. He has created us anew in Christ Jesus so we can do the good things he planned for us long ago."

Below are some foundational truths to help us trust and believe who He says we are in Christ. Although this may take a lifetime to fully grasp, these are the anchors we must hold onto when times of trouble come. When memories try to keep us stuck in the past, and steal our joy, or the world tries to get us to doubt our faith in who He says we are in Christ, we must remind ourselves of the truth in the scriptures:

- I am a child of God. I am loved. God loves me. I am valuable. He sacrificed his Son for me. He wants to be with me forever. He made me wonderfully and with honor. I am His handiwork. He gives me talents to discover, develop, use, and enjoy for His glory. He satisfies me with good things. In all things, He is working for my good. He chooses me and appoints me to bear fruit; I can ask Him for whatever I need.[4]

- I am seen and known by God. He knows my temperament, what makes me laugh and cry. He sees me when I sleep and when I rise. He watches over me. He has unique plans for me. He has prepared good things for me to do. He's given me all my roles: daughter, wife, mom, sister, and friend. He knows me inside and out. He created me just as I am, in His image. He lives in me through the Holy Spirit! I am a magnificent creation made for extraordinary purposes.[5]

- He is with me through my joy and pain. When I suffer, He suffers. When I rejoice, He rejoices. He never forsakes me. When I don't know what to say, He gives me the words. When I need to stay quiet, He gives me wisdom, strength, and self-control.[6]

- He is patient and kind to me. He knows what I need and what's best for me even before I ask Him. I am royalty, a chosen person. He allows hard times to benefit me. My current pain is temporary. It helps me empathize with others who may be undergoing the same experience.[7]

- I am a new creation! His love for me covers all my sins: past, present, and future. He nailed my sins to the cross when He died for me. He sees me as not guilty. He doesn't treat me as I deserve. He does not condemn me. I am free, no longer a slave to sin. When I sin, I confess it so I can continue to walk in the light and receive His forgiveness. His blood continually washes away my sins. He knows my weaknesses. I have true riches. I have His favor.[8]

- He calls me His friend. He tells me and entrusts me with His Master's business. Everything He learned from his Father He has made known to me. He satisfies me with good things. He is trustworthy. I can trust Him.[9]
- I have a Savior. I can't do it on my own. Nobody can be my Savior except Jesus. He is perfect. I am not. God sees the righteousness of Jesus when He sees me. I am more than a conqueror. No one can snatch me out of God's hands. I am a victor, not a victim. Nothing can separate me from God's love. He is always with me. I am never alone.[10]
- I am grateful for my life. I am living my best life in Christ. I make mistakes. He loves me anyway. I set my mind on the things above. This world is not my home. I have citizenship in Heaven. I don't compare my life to others,' or the gifts He gives each of us. I am a part of God's plan. I am satisfied with my portion. My portion spills over. He is my great provider and my great reward. I have everything I need for life and godliness.[11]
- I have fellowship with other believers who are my brothers and sisters. I am accepted and belong to His family. We are all members of His body, the Kingdom of God. We are a unit with different skills, purposes, and spiritual gifts. We each have a role to play. No part is better than the other. If one-part hurts, we all hurt. When one part celebrates, we all celebrate.[12]

I pray you let these truths sink deep down and take root in your heart and mind so you can hold onto them in your time of need. Take the time you need to reflect on them before moving on.

I digress back to my school year, and how God answered my prayer. It wasn't in the way I expected.

He placed me in a position that I enjoyed and suited my strengths. I helped to discover my students' gifts and strengths, and the careers that would suit them in the future. I also got my pay increase, and a room with a desk! But here's what I didn't expect. The position required me to collaborate with different people that would expose my weaknesses in areas He wanted me to grow in. And grow, I did. *Thank you, Lord.*

Questions

1. We come from broken pasts, which can cloud our perception of who we are in Christ. Is there trauma from the past keeping you from believing all He says you are in Christ? What can you do to change this?

_____
_____
_____
_____

2. Can you think of a love song that depicts your relationship with God? If so, write it down here and plan to listen to it this week. Try making it your love song between the two of you and see if it doesn't bring you to a deeper level of worship. (Some other good ones are Barry White's, My First, My Last, My Everything[13], Brian Adams, (Everything I Do), I do it for You[14], and John Legend's, All of Me.[15]

_____
_____
_____
_____

3. In addition to the foundational truths listed at the end of this chapter, look up 2 or 3 additional scriptures that speak to your heart about your identity in Christ. Write them down on index cards or other creative way and review it regularly to remind yourself of who you are in Him.

_____
_____
_____
_____

Reflection

At my place of employment, I treated others the way they treated me. Even when it was wrong. This was my weakness. God placed me in a position where I needed to communicate directly with people who challenged me in this area. As a result, when I prayed for a peaceful and supportive working environment it was not given until I changed my ways first.

When I decided to repent, I not only was at peace with myself and my Maker, but I also had no expectations of reciprocation from my colleagues. However, by years end as I became more supportive of my co-workers, they became more supportive of me.

Is there a relationship in your life that you need to repent in? What will you do differently even if they don't change?

_____

_____

_____

_____

God's Promise

Because of Christ and our faith in Him, we can now come fearlessly into God's presence, assured of his glad welcome.

Ephesians 3:12

As Christians, we can doubt that God wants to give us His best, to prosper us and not harm us, to give us hope and a future. Our fears concerning this influence the choices we make and can impact our relationships and the plans He has for us.

What dreams would you chase if you genuinely believed you would prosper and not fail? In what ways would you act differently in your relationships with others?

_____

_____

_____

_____

Chapter One - Verse Find
Proverbs 3:5-6

"Trust in the Lord with all your heart and lean not on your own understanding; in all your ways submit to him and he will make your paths straight."

```
T  E  S  D  L  T  O  W  U  A  W  R  S  V  B
R  K  B  H  L  B  C  O  M  F  I  K  U  S  G
G  C  P  O  Q  G  O  T  R  U  S  T  V  B  G
X  G  E  F  U  H  D  W  C  N  U  O  W  U  I
M  I  R  L  P  G  X  D  I  D  B  T  D  O  T
U  C  L  E  F  U  D  P  Z  E  M  B  O  U  X
W  A  Y  S  J  R  X  F  O  R  I  S  S  E  K
L  T  D  O  G  Z  Q  H  M  S  T  T  X  Y  X
D  D  Q  N  U  L  A  E  A  T  R  R  Y  R  H
K  G  W  L  O  R  D  U  K  A  H  A  X  N  T
G  O  P  A  E  T  X  U  E  N  B  I  Y  D  I
A  Z  Y  F  P  A  T  H  S  D  E  G  W  S  A
D  L  R  H  X  Q  N  T  G  I  X  H  K  U  D
Q  M  F  S  G  J  R  X  A  N  C  T  B  F  M
D  A  F  A  L  D  O  O  U  G  D  M  W  M  J
```

TRUST	LEAN	ALL	MAKE	YOUR
LORD	NOT	OWN	WAYS	PATHS
HEART	UNDERSTANDING		SUBMIT	

Chapter Two

Trials Produce Hope

"Not only so, but we also glory in our sufferings because we know that suffering produces perseverance; perseverance, character; and character, hope. And hope does not put us to shame because God's love has been poured out into our hearts through the Holy Spirit, who has been given to us."

Romans 5:3-5

I hung up the phone with my 23-year-old son, Zach, feeling defeated. We were not in conflict, but he was feeling discouraged. He shared with me the difficulties he was having in his young life, his relationship problems, his need for character change, his questioning of his next business venture, and his uncertainty about where he should settle.

Sitting on the couch, I thought about each of my three sons and decided to pray. *Lord, You have a plan for Zach, Harry, and Hunter. Guide them along clear paths to help them find their way. Help me be a good listener so they can figure it out by themselves. Help them to feel supported and encouraged by me and not criticized or judged. You know the plans You have for them. Help me get out of the way so they may seek*

Your direction. Comfort them and show them which way to go. Thank You for watching over them all the days of their lives. In Jesus's name. Amen.

It's hard to stand by and watch my kids struggle. I just want to reach in and make everything better. But without persevering through their difficulties, they'll never develop maturity or have the character and convictions God wants for them.

Romans 5:3-5 says we should rejoice in our sufferings because our suffering produces perseverance, character, and hope. Hope is what keeps us going when life gets uncertain. I need it, and my kids need it.

So, despite the hurt in my heart, I prayed, gave it to God, trusted He was working powerfully in my son's life, and got back to what I was doing.

Expect Trials

Have you ever resolved to start a budget, but then your car broke down, and you gave up the plan because you had to spend the money on new tires instead? In the same way, Jesus promised that in this life, we would have troubles.[1] Some of us walk the Christian life expecting it to be all sunshine and roses. Then when something terrible happens, we give up on our goals or worse, give up on God. It's just like living on a budget where we prepare ourselves for unexpected expenses by saving money in an emergency fund, we need to expect trials and learn how to persevere through them to reach our goals.

Rejoice in Sufferings

When trouble comes, we must learn to hold onto our faith and believe God is still working for our good. When we see trouble as an agent for God to build our character, we can rejoice through our difficulties, even if it takes some time to get to that place of surrender. If we don't understand what trials do for us, we do all kinds of soul-numbing things to drown out our sufferings.

If we adopt an attitude of rejoicing in our troubles, we live by faith and not by sight.[2] When we can be joyful through our momentary troubles, we choose to believe God is still with us, is fully aware of them, and is working on our behalf for His glory through them. We honor God by rejoicing through our difficulties. We don't pretend the problem doesn't exist, but we take our concerns to Him. For those who may need help doing this, I offer you what I typically do:

- First, pray; talk aloud, go for a walk, or journal, and tell God your trouble; ask Him to guide you.
- Get with a trusted friend, mentor, or advisor who can listen and give advice and perspective.
- Write down things you will do or solutions that come to mind.
- Be mindful about what Jesus would do in this situation.
- Wait until the right time to act, then do it.
- Reflect on the answer and repeat the first step until you are at peace with your problem.

When I handle my problems this way, I grow and glorify God as he works for my good. He promises I will reap a harvest if I do not give up.[3] We can keep going after a little while with the Lord!

Seek to Understand

As we live, work, and go to school in community with others, we will experience conflicts. It's inevitable. I used to avoid confrontation at all costs, but I've since learned to embrace it as it allows me to help another person understand me as I seek to understand them.

Having this mind-shift of seeking to understand another person, especially when having bad feelings towards them, gives the opportunity for your relationship to grow. When we can listen to and accept another person without judgment of who and where they are along their journey, we establish trust with another individual.

When we don't do this the tension between us builds, bad feelings are harbored in our hearts, and our relationships break down.

How often do we try to get our point across rather than listen to another person's point of view? What if we asked questions to help understand a person instead of judging or assuming what their motives were? This is especially difficult to do when we are feeling hurt. But staying curious about the other person's viewpoint will help in understanding.

Proverbs 18:2 states, "Fools find no pleasure in understanding, but delight in airing their own opinions." Let's listen to other people, gain perspective, and build up relationships.

My Wretched Old Self

Before I became a Christian, I worked in New York City, made a bundle of money, and lived in an apartment with a view overlooking the Hudson River. I worked hard at appearing to have it all together. I was fit, wore expensive clothing, and drove a fancy sports car. But on the inside, I was insecure, directionless and a people pleaser.

MaryAnn with the People

In my relationships, I would do and say anything just to keep the peace. But behind their backs I would badmouth them to anyone who would listen to me.

Oh, how I hated who I was.

To tell you I was lost, and without a sense of self or purpose was an understatement. I was phony, self-righteous, and indecisive, all at the same time.

At times I felt superior to others and was perceived as arrogant; other times, I felt inferior and avoided people altogether in my own little protected world. Honestly, I shudder to think about what my life would be like if I hadn't become a Christian.

Jesus with the People

Jesus's approach to relationships was quite different than mine. He knew who He was and what He came to do. When He was about twelve, He went about His purpose by separating himself from His family and staying back in Jerusalem during Passover. At the same time, His mother and father frantically searched for him. They found him three days later in the temple courts listening to the teachers and asking them questions.[4]

He prioritized God as first in His life and spent time alone with Him in prayer,[5] He allowed Himself to be led and directed by the Holy Spirit.[6] Because He humbled himself and became an image of a man,[7] He had deep compassion for His creation and empathy towards humankind. He knew man's need for connection, so He kept His companions close to him even though they weren't much help to Him.[8] He challenged the self-righteous,[9] helped the widows,[10] had compassion on the poor,[11] healed those with spiritual and physical afflictions,[12] sought after the lost,[13] and so on.

Through the stories recorded in the Bible, Jesus soon became my hero because He loved the unlovable, namely me. And He showed me how to love others and manage all the different relationships in my life.

The most awe-inspiring interactions were Jesus's confrontations with the teachers of the law, the Pharisees. He knew what was inside of them, but He loved them anyway. He was bold and spoke the truth to them. He was not afraid or offended by their insults. Instead, He completely entrusted Himself to God.

When He spoke to people, He focused in on the part of their heart that needed attention. To the man at the pool in Bethesda who had lost hope and settled by living his 38 years of life with an infirmity, He asked him, "Do you want to get well?" Afterward, Jesus followed up with him at the temple, and gave him the antidote to complete his healing. "See, you are well again. Stop sinning, or something worse may happen to you."[14]

He knew why He was here and went about His purpose with conviction. When He began His public ministry, He read the Messianic prophecy to the people from Isaiah 61:1-2 stating confidently, "Today this Scripture is fulfilled in your hearing." Infuriated, the angry crowd wanted to push him off the cliff, but he walked right past them. He knew His time had not yet come.[15]

Jesus didn't get angry at people. Not even at the Pharisees. His righteous indignation was directed towards the peoples' actions. We know this because the scriptures say that having anger at someone is equivocal to harboring murder in the heart,[16] and Jesus was about loving and saving people, not killing them. *Praise God.*

When the chief priests and elders accused Him, He did not answer.[17] He had the wisdom to keep His mouth shut. When insulted, He didn't lash back; when He suffered, He did not threaten to harm anyone. Instead, He entrusted Himself to God, the just judge of all things.[18]

Jesus's example of how He approached people and interacted with them is one I aspire to emulate all my days.

Questions

1. How has your perspective of going through trials changed after reading Romans 5:3-5? Is there a trial you or your loved one is going through now that you see differently?

_____

_____

_____

_____

2. In your own words, what does it mean to seek to understand someone else's viewpoint? Is there a relationship in your life where you need to apply this?

_____

_____

_____

_____

3. Jesus loved all people but responded to them differently. What is the key to dealing with all kinds of people? Which example of how Jesus loved people is most challenging to imitate?

_____

_____

_____

_____

Reflection

I am in awe of Jesus' life. He preached the good news to the brokenhearted. He bound up the captives. He stayed away from money, and being poor didn't bother Him. When He saw people in need in the land, He told the rich people to give them money. _Amazing!_

Lord, you know all things, including the hearts, and the lives of the people around us. We live in the United States of America and are rich beyond measure compared to the rest of the world. Show us how we can be effective with what You've given us, as Jesus *did with the people. Give us a heart of compassion. Show us our neighbors who are spiritually or monetarily hurting, who are sick, or in need of provisions. Guide us to those souls who are willing to accept our help. You have given us so much. We want to imitate Jesus and give to others in need. In His name, Amen.*

Write your own prayer asking God to show you how you can help others with what He's given you.

_____

_____

_____

_____

God's Promise

"Consider it pure joy, my brothers and sisters, whenever you face trials of many kinds because you know that the testing of your faith produces perseverance. Let perseverance finish its work so that you may be mature and complete, not lacking anything."

James 1:2-4

Joy and trials don't seem to go together. Yet God's Word tells us otherwise. How can you think of problems differently, with pure pleasure instead of dread? How do trials make us mature and complete, not lacking anything?

_____

_____

_____

_____

Chapter Two - Crossword Puzzle
Directions: Use the Clues Below to Complete the Crossword Puzzle that Contain the Words in Romans 5:3-5

"Not only so, but we also glory in our sufferings, because we know that suffering produces perseverance; perseverance, character; and character hope. And hope does not put us to shame, because God's love has been poured out into our hearts through the Holy Spirit, who has been given to us."

Across

5. Defeated or degraded state visible to those around you

6. Presented as a gift

9. Persistence in doing something despite difficulty or delay in achieving success

10. To flow out or gush forth

Down

1. Undergoing pain, distress, or hardships

2. Confident expectations and desire for something good in the future

3. Qualities of an individual

4. The third person of the Trinity

6. God's presence as perceived by humans

7. To bring forward

8. Emotional nature and understanding

Chapter Two Crossword Puzzle

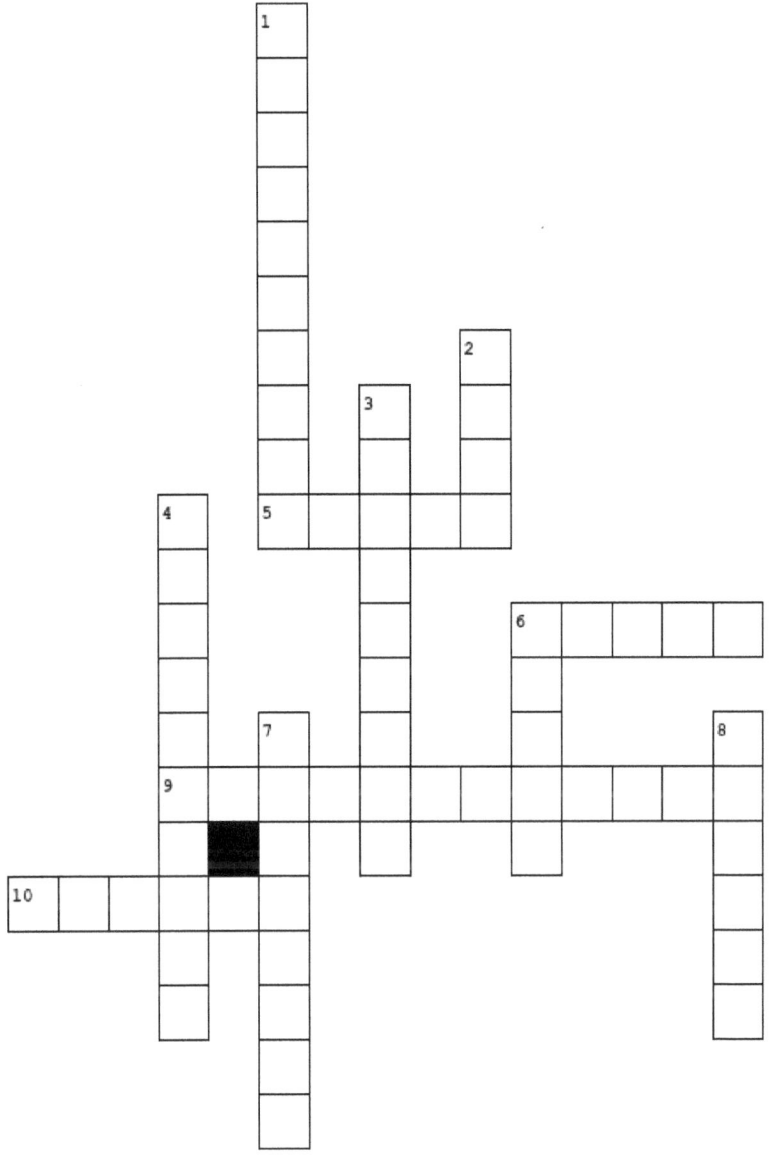

Chapter Three

Surrender

"Come to me, all you who are weary and burdened, and I will give you rest. Take my yoke upon you and learn from me, for I am gentle and humble in heart, and you will find rest for your souls. For my yoke is easy and my burden is light."

Matthew 11:28-30

It started as a perfect Sunday.

I woke up early, slipped my New Balance sneakers on my feet, put my Apple Beats in my ears, and sprang out the door in eager anticipation for a brisk morning jog.

My feet pelted the pavement at 161 beats per minute to Michael Sembello's, *Maniac*.[1] I felt happy and alive.

I took a new route down the main road near our house that led to an overlook with a river below. Jogging in place, I peered through the wired fence hoping to spot the bear I had seen in the neighborhood two weeks before. Seeing no signs of wildlife, I hopped across a grassy verge that separated the sidewalk from the road. Suddenly, my right ankle turned and gave way beneath me. To keep myself upright and save myself from falling, I twisted my back, which popped two of my ribs. Finally, I stumbled to the ground in defeat.

As I struggled to get up, I heard a voice saying, "Are you okay? Do you want me to drive you home?" I looked up to see a middle-aged woman in her vehicle pulled up beside me. She must have seen the whole thing.

Embarrassed, I said, "No thanks, I'm going to walk it off." And the kind-hearted stranger drove away.

As I plodded on my way, my ribs began to ache, and my ankle started to throb. *How much damage could I have done?* I thought to myself.

When I arrived home, the pain intensified to the point I could no longer walk, and I made my way to the couch and sat down. Hearing my husband in the kitchen, I called out to him, "*We need to go to the emergency room.*"

The x-rays showed I had fractured my lateral malleolus, or the fibula, the bone on the outside of the ankle. In addition, I was sure I broke a couple of ribs, but the technician told me there was not much you could do about them, so we never had them looked at.

A Call to Slow Down

God has a sense of humor. Just the day before, I told my Saturday morning breakfast club how difficult it was for me to slow down. There was so much I wanted to do. Write, market, and publish, my book, sell merchandise, create, read, travel, explore, and otherwise, you know, live my life.

But God allowed this setback for my good. It was the perfect opportunity for me to step back and assess how I was living. It was a call to live differently, more mindfully.

Coincidently, I was reading John Mark Comer's, *The Ruthless Elimination of Hurry* in which he discusses the importance of slowing down not only on the Sabbath, but the other six days, too. Here's an excerpt from his book:

We work, play, cook, clean, shop, exercise, text, and inhabit the modern world all week, but finally, we hit a limit. On the Sabbath, we slow down; more than that, we come to a complete stop.

One of the surprising things I learned when I began to really practice Sabbath is that to enjoy the seventh day, you have to slow down the other six days. You can't go ninety miles per hour all week running the pedal to the floor, harrowing your soul to the bone for six days straight, and then expect to slam on the brakes for Sabbath and immediately feel Zen awesome. You have to find the rhythm. As we used to say when I played indie rock bands, "Find the Pocket."

Because the Sabbath isn't just a twenty-four-hour time slot in your weekly schedule; it's a spirit of restfulness that goes with you throughout your week. A way of working from rest, not for rest, with nothing to prove. A way of bearing fruit from abiding, not ambition.[2]

Before Comer's revelation, I thought a good rhythm of life was striving, accompanied by feelings of anxiety, too much to do, and insufficient time to do it in. Living in this "restless" state, I tried to make things happen to prove myself worthy. Instead, God called me to rest, or abide in knowing who I am in Christ. He wanted me to accept His calling with a sense of ease and pleasure. *Thank you, Lord.*

During the healing of my ankle, I had no choice but to slow down and surrender my plans and schedule to God. It was clearly His will for me.

As I listened and sought His direction, He guided me daily. Not only did I find time to work on my book, but I wasn't rushing when I wrote. I was relaxed, carefree and enjoyed the process. I took the time to discern which stories I felt He wanted me to include. I also figured out that I would write my book while working at my teaching job, so I still had an income. I decided when I was finished, I would wait for Him to show me what to do next.

Surrender

Some days were easier than others. One day, I sat on my sofa, feeling powerless. I couldn't do my exercise routine and feared losing the fitness level I had attained prior to my accident. I knew I had to rely on God in a deeper way.

According to Merriam-Webster, surrender means to give oneself up into the power of another. Trusting God had the plan for my life, was guiding me, and knowing I could rest in that was what He wanted for me. My body needed a real rest, a soul kind of rest. Changing habits took time. Putting my life into His hands required relinquishment of control. Often, I desired to return to the old way of doing things my way. It would be three more weeks until my next doctor's appointment, when they told me I'd be healed enough to become more independent. Sometimes I felt like kicking and screaming. I even cried a time or two, but none of that changed my situation. So instead, I would pray, *Your will be done, not my own.*

I read my Bible. Even more on difficult days. I was growing my faith muscles as I chose to accept my situation. I trained my mind to stop worrying, and instead, I listened to what He was telling me to do. *Let go of trying to make things happen for yourself, your plans, and your agenda, MaryAnn. Listen to My Words and put into practice what They say. Claim them for yourself. Learn from Me, My yoke is easy, and My burden is light.*

One morning. I woke up at 5 a.m. to sit and watch the sunrise on my enclosed front porch to see and listen to nature. I observed baby foxes scrambling with one another across my front lawn and bumble bees eating their breakfasts at the blooming Rose of Sharon bushes.

I sat in awe as the hummingbirds zipped from one flower to the other. Hovering over the bicolored white and red hibiscuses, they darted in for a quick meal, and disappeared as fast as they came. Do you know their heart's beat at 1,260/minute during the warm season? And on cold nights, they drop down to 50-180 beats/minute, which for them is a state of hibernation.[3]

God has a plan for them. He takes care of them. They do not spin and worry. They go about their work glorifying Him as they go. I can do the same.

On day one, I sat only for twenty minutes. The next day it was thirty. Later, I'd look at my watch and notice I've been watching from my perch for an hour. The minutes passed quickly as the players took their roles in nature's grand performance; before I knew it, it was 6 a.m.

Like clockwork, the neighbor's sprinkler turned on and cars began motoring down the street. A pang of sadness swept over me because I knew my time of solace had ended. It was time to go back inside the house.

There is something special, magical even, about being up before the rest of the world. Alone by myself, I can listen to and discern my thoughts. I can decide which ones to hold onto and which ones to let go. I ponder their messages and discover their meanings. I've learned to bring a notepad and pencil with me during these moments. Then I can jot down what I plan to do for the day as my priorities begin to take shape.

My Plans Vs. God's Plans

I'm a dreamer and an achiever. My husband is a "let's play it by ear" kind of guy. God knew what He was doing when He brought us together. Between the two of us, we've got a healthier balance of both worlds.

It's important to make goals for ourselves, but we need to bring those plans to God to discern if He's putting them there or if we are forcing our agendas on Him. Ideally, we should be working with God.

When I ask God for guidance, He often answers me through other people and by opening and closing doors. My questions also may be met with silence. In this case, I may be in a period of waiting. He also communicates with me through the fellowship of others, sermon messages, personal Bible studies, and the Spirit's promptings.

Have you ever decided to give someone a call just because they came to your mind? Most likely this is the Spirit's prompting. Often, when I am in a quiet space, I think of my needs, or someone else's, and scriptures come to mind for our encouragement.

The more we are in our Bibles, the more we can discern what is Truth and what is not. When we follow the Spirit's promptings and act on the good He's calling us to do we can discern which are the Words of God and which are the lies of Satan. Any thoughts or actions contrary to Jesus's teachings are not from the Spirit of God.[4]

The Seasons of Life

In this life, we have seasons. Just as plants act differently in summer and winter, we must learn to modulate our activities from one season to the next. Reflecting over a year, we can see the bigger picture, not just what's happening day-to-day.

If we are in a time of waiting, we can surrender our plans to His timing because we can trust Him. He has an eternal perspective and the best directions for us to go.

One of my favorite scriptures is Ecclesiastes 3:1-8. The teacher has the following to say about our times and seasons:

There is a time for everything,
and a season for every activity under the heavens:

a time to be born and a time to die,
a time to plant and a time to uproot,
a time to kill and a time to heal,
a time to tear down and a time to build,
a time to weep and a time to laugh,
a time to mourn and a time to dance,
a time to scatter stones and a time to gather them,
a time to embrace and a time to refrain from embracing,
a time to search and a time to give up,
a time to keep and a time to throw away,
a time to tear and a time to mend,
a time to be silent and a time to speak,
a time to love and a time to hate,
a time for war and a time for peace.[5]

I'm from northern New Jersey. We have distinct seasons: summer, fall, winter, and spring. In other parts of the world, the seasons may seem more the same.

Most of us in the modern world have grocery stores, electricity, and motorized vehicles. Because of these conveniences, we don't think much about the seasons, and the need to plant and harvest. We tend to do the same things year after year, never changing our routines.

The Farmer

But for the farmer, each season required different tasks to be performed. They relied on the seasons for their food, and livelihood. What they did in one season differed greatly from what they did in another.

In spring, they plowed the fields and planted their seeds. In summer, they grew and tended their crops. Fall was the time for harvest. Winter was a time to plan for the following year. Like the farmer, our seasons change according to our needs and life's happenings.

Maybe you're a teen in your first year of college and have no idea how to manage your time because your parents did it for you. Or you are single and have a full-time job, but you're staying up late with your friends as you did when you were in college. Or you recently got married and are trying to figure out how to set boundaries with your single friends. Maybe you and your husband decided to have a baby, and this bundle of love is disrupting your double income, no kids' lifestyle. Or you have teens that need your attention now more than ever, but you have no time for them because, well, aren't they supposed to be independent?

Widows, empty-nesters, and the like, we have newfound seasons that call for reflection and planning; so we can still bear fruit until the end of our lives on earth. We must put in the time, get advice and plan so we can thrive in all the seasons.

Thinking back to when I broke my ankle, I confessed to one of my friends that I felt like a fish stuck in a bowl. I felt limited in what I could do in my body, and I grudgingly went through the motions while waiting to get to heaven. But my thinking was wrong.

Thankfully, my friend wouldn't let me wallow in self-pity for long. She told me there was a time in her life when she felt like a gerbil running on a wheel, just going through the motions. Then she looked at me empathetically, smiled, and said, "But God has a plan for you. He wrote a book about your life from start to finish, and the details of each chapter in between."

I thank God for good friends. Godly friends will tell you the truth no matter what. They will take the time to pray with you if you phone them during your times of struggle.

No, my life was not over, far from it. I was in a season of life in which God was teaching me some vital lessons.

When it seems our lives have come to a complete halt, it is then we see our need for Him, and we cry out, *Lord help us!*

When all else and everyone fails us at one time or another, our relationship with Him is one we can be sure of. Soon we'll discover He really is our great reward, and the people He places in our lives are gifts for us to love.

If we are still living and breathing on this earth, He has great and wonderful plans for us. Plans to fulfill the desires of our hearts. In our times alone, in reflection and in prayer, He makes those plans known to us. But we must slow down enough to hear them, and He will continue to place them in our hearts.

Perspective

Keeping perspective is important when things don't seem to go as planned. I use a two-year calendar to remind me of the big picture. It allows me to plan my seasons, weeks, and days to ensure I'm making time for the most important things. Periodically, I will turn to the yearly pages to reflect on where I've been and where I want to go. In times of difficulty, I remember that this time is just one day in my month, year, or lifetime. And tomorrow will be a better day.

When planning my year, I like to put down my workdays and vacation times first, and then my travel plans. Then I plan the next season, month, week, and day as activities come up. I assess my needs for downtime and rest, and buffer that into my calendar, too. Of course, my plans may change as I listen and discern what God may have me do as I go.

Ecclesiastes 3:11 says, "He has made everything beautiful in its time. He has also set eternity in the human heart; yet no one can fathom what God has done from beginning to end."

We may never understand what God is accomplishing during our good and bad days on this earth, and through all the seasons, but we trust He has our good in mind, and the best plans for our lives.

Questions

1. In what areas of your life is it most challenging to relinquish control to God? Why?

_____

_____

_____

_____

2. Are you in a difficult season and don't know what to do? Write out a prayer and present your needs to God. Thank Him for what He's already given you[6] and for guiding you in your next steps. He delights in giving us peace![7]

_____

_____

_____

_____

3. Think of your worst problem right now and try looking at it from the big picture? How has doing this changed your perspective?

_____

_____

_____

_____

Reflection

Jesus said in Matthew 11:28-30, "Come to me, all you who are weary and burdened, and I will give you rest. Take my yoke upon you and learn from me, for I am gentle and humble in heart, and you will find rest for your souls. For my yoke is easy and my burden is light."

This scripture makes me think of Jesus walking alongside me, gently and humbly. He wants me to give Him my physical, emotional, and spiritual load.

When people say mean things to me and I want to lash back, I picture Jesus looking at this person with love, because He knows they are hurting. Then He looks at me and nods as if everything will be alright. Now I see this person in a different light. I know this person's pain, and my disposition softens. I realize this isn't about me; my soul is at rest. I look to Jesus, who shows me how to respond in love.

When I'm afraid to speak the truth, I look to Jesus' example and gain newfound courage and I speak what is true in love.

By myself, I am weak, but I look to Him because He has overcome the world. With Him, so can I. I trust He can manage my burdens. My victory comes from Him alone. Even when I fail, He is by my side, always helping and guiding.

What does 'yoked to Jesus' mean to you? What behavior(s) can you learn from Jesus?

_____

_____

_____

_____

God's Promise

My Father's house has many rooms; if that were not so, would I have told you that I
am going there to prepare a place for you?

John 14:2

How does this scripture help you understand the big picture of God's plans
for your life?

_____

_____

_____

_____

Chapter Three - Verse Find
Ecclesiastes 3:1, 3:6b (MSG)

"There is a time for everything, and a season for every activity under the heavens...a time to hold on and a time to let go."

```
M  U  G  L  V  H  M  T  U  A  N  K  F  S  X
R  A  V  Q  K  P  V  E  L  Q  Z  I  N  U  Z
R  P  I  T  M  Y  R  V  V  H  S  P  Y  C  S
B  B  F  E  W  Z  L  E  M  E  O  U  P  C  O
C  H  R  U  N  D  E  R  I  A  R  L  P  M  M
U  R  T  D  L  F  T  Y  Q  V  S  Y  D  T  G
Y  A  C  T  I  V  I  T  Y  E  K  W  O  S  O
U  G  L  D  I  C  M  H  H  N  F  C  N  T  R
F  H  I  C  C  L  E  I  I  S  A  H  X  T  Z
F  H  R  G  V  E  O  N  F  A  J  S  X  C  E
J  D  S  K  O  L  A  G  X  L  Y  N  M  X  V
I  L  G  R  S  E  A  S  O  N  H  W  M  L  X
B  L  B  J  Y  T  H  E  R  E  I  S  H  M  K
F  Y  S  I  P  Q  S  X  W  N  H  U  E  I  A
V  U  U  S  L  A  Q  S  M  C  H  I  F  B  P
```

THERE	SEASON	UNDER	ON
TIME `	EVERY	HEAVENS	LET
EVERYTHING	ACTIVITY	HOLD	GO

.

Part 2

The Power

Living powerful and effective lives as Christians is quite different than what it means by the world's standards. Rather than act on our impulses, we read our Bibles, pray, and get advice. We submit to one another, seek His guidance, and wait for Him to open doors. We don't strive, take matters into our own hands, or grasp our way to the top. When we are insulted, we don't take revenge. On the contrary, we bless, serve, and go the extra mile with our enemies. Sounds fun? Not always, but we trust God is working for our good, the good of others, and for His ultimate plans.

Thought Questions

1. How does God's Word hold Power? In what ways do our feelings lie to us?

2. What does it mean "When I am weak, then I am strong? Why do we need a Savior?

3. How do we remain righteous when we make mistakes? How does living righteously affect our prayer life?

Chapter Four

Humility

"That is why, for Christ's sake, I delight in weaknesses, in insults, in hardships, in persecutions, in difficulties. For when I am weak, then I am strong."

2 Corinthians 12:10

I came home from work feeling defeated. The enemy was lurking in the forefront of my mind trying to discourage me with feelings of inadequacy, unimportance, and belief I was failing at my profession.

Enough! Lord, please come quickly with your Words of Truth. I cannot fight this battle on my own. Help me remember that the battle is Yours. That You gave me this job no matter how insignificant I feel in it, and You will help me do it well. Help me remember the value You place on my life. Then I lay on the couch and drifted off to sleep.

Several minutes later, my son woke me and asked if we could order pizza for dinner earlier than we had planned.

"Let's do it!" I said emphatically. "I'm hungry!"

My son dialed the number to our favorite pizzeria shop in town and twenty minutes later, we ate a delicious meal of pepperoni pizza, garlic knots, fried calamari, and asparagus.

It's wonderful how satisfying food and a well-timed nap can change a bad mood from gloomy to renewed in no time. It was just what I needed to strengthen and encourage me to continue on.

But what if I had reacted and said or did something I would have later regretted? Psalm 40:1-3 says that waiting on the Lord until the testing subsides is a better option.

> *"I waited patiently for the Lord;*
> *He turned to me and heard my cry.*
> *He lifted me out of the slimy pit,*
> *out of the mud and mire;*
> *He set my feet on a rock*
> *and gave me a firm place to stand.*
> *He put a new song in my mouth,*
> *a hymn of praise to our God.*
> *Many will see and fear the Lord*
> *and put their trust in him.*

Paul didn't say in 2 Corinthians 12:10, *if* I am weak, he said *when* I am weak. He knew his weaknesses and we should know ours, too. God certainly knows them and remembers we are flesh and blood. He knows we will have trouble in this world.[1] We will have struggles. But Jesus said He would be with us in our weaknesses, and that His grace is sufficient for us. He has overcome the world, and He said in time He would lift us up.[2]

Everlasting God

I couldn't get the song out of my head; it's called Everlasting God. I heard it at church last Sunday and have been playing it daily on my morning jog ever since. I love the Lincoln Brewster[3] version of the song. In the end, a little child's voice recites Isaiah 40:28-31, which states:

> *"Do you not know?*
> *Have you not heard?*
> *The Lord is the everlasting God,*
> *the Creator of the ends of the earth.*

He will not grow tired or weary,
and his understanding no one can fathom.
He gives strength to the weary
and increases the power of the weak.
Even youths grow tired and weary,
and young men stumble and fall;
but those who hope in the Lord
will renew their strength.
They will soar on wings like eagles;
they will run and not grow weary,
they will walk and not be faint."

Power in Weakness

Dear friends, I cannot stress this point enough. When we are weak, then we are strong. Until we embrace our weaknesses, accept them, admit them, and yes, continually repent of them, it is then we can be strong because we will receive Christ's power to overcome them.

The Beatitudes remind us that the meek shall inherit the earth and the Kingdom of Heaven belongs to the poor in spirit.[4] When we understand who we are as imperfect, and wretched apart from Him, we will cry out to Him, and He will help us in our time of need.[5] When we are humble with God, in our relationships with others, and humble with ourselves, we will begin to understand the power of God.

We must remember who we are in our sinful nature, that we are saved sinners who rely on our Savior every day. We are souls with bodies that return to dust until the day we are called home to our permanent residence in heaven.

Pride in Disguise

In his December 2008 Reflections, C.S. Lewis stated the following about pride:

"According to Christian teachers, Pride is the essential vice, the utmost evil. Unchastity, anger, greed, drunkenness, and all that, are mere flea bites in comparison: it was through pride that the devil became the devil: Pride leads to

every other vice: it is the complete anti-God state of mind is Pride which has been the chief cause of misery in every nation and every family since the world began.

Does this seem to you exaggerated? If so, think it over. I pointed out a moment ago that the more pride one had, the more one disliked pride in others. In fact, if you want to find out how proud you are the easiest way is to ask yourself, "How much do I dislike it when other people snub me, or refuse to take any notice of me, or shove their oar in, or patronize me, or show off?" The point is that each person's pride is in competition with everyone else's pride. It is because I wanted to be the big noise at the party that I am so annoyed at someone else being the big noise."⁶

On the opposite side of the coin, pride is not only characterized as arrogant and boastful but as a person who has low self-esteem!

Dr. Anna Schaffner, Professor of Cultural History at Kent University, described the person with a negative sense of self just as prideful as someone with a narcissistic overvaluation of their talents. She stated, "Extremely low self-esteem...lacks accuracy [and is] just an inverted form of self-obsession, another way of fixating on ourselves rather than directing our attention towards others."⁷

She continued, "We begin to do this by accurately understanding our strengths and weaknesses. Then we must *own our imperfections*. When we do, we no longer waste our energy hiding them from others but can seek to learn to live with them productively or even to overcome them."⁸

Pride in Action

I decided to take a break from my writing to mow the lawn. As I stepped outside my back deck to go start the mower, I saw my neighbor in her yard. After our exchange of a friendly "hello," and "how are you?," our light conversation turned into a prideful and defensive battlefield in my mind because I felt misunderstood.

Why did I have to share so much information with her about my son? She must think I'm a terrible mom because he must get his friends to drive him home from practice and not me. Was I boasting about him too much?

And on and on I went ruminating over what I should and shouldn't have said.

Be quick to listen, slow to speak, and slow to get angry,[9] I said to myself. *What a wretched woman I am. Lord, forgive me."*

Then I vowed to listen and pray for wisdom the next time I spoke with her again. Then I let it go.

What is Humility?

According to Shaffner, Humility is an attitude of spiritual modesty that comes from understanding our place in the larger order of things. Derived from the word humus, or earth, it clashes with our current valuation of self-worth and self-realization; it calls for not taking our desires, successes, or failings too seriously.[10]

David Mathis, the editor of Desiring God and pastor of Cities Church, writes, "Humility entails a right view of self, as created by and accountable to God, which requires a right view of God, as Creator and authoritative in relation to his creatures. Humility is not, then, preoccupied with self, and one's lowliness, but first mindful of and conscious of God, and his highness, and then of self in respect to him."[11]

True Humility

Knowing who we are and who God is, is of first importance if we are to become genuinely humble. When we know our place as the *created, not The Creator*, the power of God will begin to shine through our lives as He fulfills His purposes for us. Hint: they may be the desires of our hearts, too, as we walk with Him.

Mathis describes it this way: "The humility of Christ shows us that true humility is not the denigrating of humanity, but God's image shining in its fullness. To humble oneself is not to be less than human. Rather, it is pride that is the cancer, pride that corrodes our true dignity. To humble ourselves is to come ever closer, step by step, to the bliss and full flourishing for which we were made."[12]

Did you catch that? It is pride that corrodes our true dignity. The world, as usual, has it upside down. When we are haughty, we are not in a place of power but weakness because God opposes us when we are in this state. But when we humble ourselves before Him, as Scripture says, "He will lift (us) up in due time."[13] In other words, God's power is with us when we submit ourselves as the created, not the creator of our lives. *Praise God.*

The Humility of Jesus

Jesus was not self-focused; instead, He focused on His Father's love for Him, His love for us, and the mission God gave Him to do. That is, save the world through Him. And He was passionate and determined enough to complete it.

Philippians 2:6-8 says, He, "Who, being in very nature God, did not consider equality with God something to be used to his own advantage; rather, he made himself nothing by taking the very nature of a servant, being made in human likeness."

Jesus humbled Himself by taking on the appearance of a man, He went from Creator to created, becoming obedient to death, and even death on a cross![14] Because He emptied Himself, "God exalted Him to the highest place and gave Him the name that is above every name, that at the name of Jesus, every knee should bow, in heaven and on earth and under the earth."[15]

When we submit to God and the purposes for which He made us, even if we have uncertainty at the time, He will lead us day by day through the uncertain times. When we submit to one another out of reverence for Christ,[16] He gives us the victory with Him, and our joy soon follows.

We must change our mindsets to love and desire humility when we think pride is the better way to act. Remember, pride is weakness. Humility is powerful. It's the upside-down way of God. It's our way to tap into His power as His vessel to achieve His purposes and our true heart's desire.

Because humility is critical to living a powerful life in Christ, I've included a table here with examples of common scenarios in which we, as humans, can get it wrong.

Examples of Prideful & Humble Responses

Scenario	Prideful Responses/ Rely on Human Weakness	Humble Responses/ Rely on God's Strength
1. Someone you care about insults you. What do you do?	a. You insult them back. b. You talk about them behind their back. c. You do nothing and let your bitterness toward them build.	a. You try to engage them in a conversation about why they felt that way. You apologize if needed. b. If not warranted, ask them if everything with them is okay. c. You pray for them.
2. You're at a party and someone is making fun of another person who is not in the room. What do you do?	a. You laugh at their remarks. b. You add your own negative talk about the person. c. You don't do anything but keep listening.	a. You stand up for the person. b. You say something positive about the person. c. You leave the conversation.
3.You have hatred in your heart towards one of your classmates/ coworkers. What do you do?	a. You allow it to harbor in your heart. b. You ignore the person without dealing with the issue. c. You say bad things about the person.	a. You pray to forgive this person. b. You give this person their favorite beverage from your local coffee shop. c. You find ways to treat them the way you'd like to be treated.

Now it's time to think of your own scenario below:

Scenario	Prideful Responses/ Rely on Human Weakness	Humble Responses/ Rely on God's Strength
1.	a. b. c.	a. b. c.

When we abide in Jesus, submit to God's ways, and do not conform to the pattern of the world, He sees us as righteous. Then we can work together with God in His infinite power to work in unimaginable ways in ours and others' lives.

Maybe God will work in our adversary's heart to soften it. Or He'll orchestrate a string of events where we end up losing a job but getting a position we've always wanted. Or we don't get the salary increase but we learn how to budget our money and still get to do what we love. Even if none of these things happen, we will have pleased our Father in Heaven, and helped to glorify His name.

The Humility of Nature

When I'm in nature, I can't help but think about God's creative work; how He made the trees grow and produce fruit and flowers. I wonder how the animals find their food, their mates, and instinctually survive in the wilderness. I ponder the tides of the ocean that rise and fall during the different lunar cycles, just as He directed them. They don't need instructions. It's as if they are pre-programmed to do what they do.

Humans are different. We were created in His Image, but we have minds of our own. Nature has an easier time submitting to their Maker than we do. When we become fearful and insecure about our lives and take matters into our own hands, we miss out on the power, love, and self-discipline He wants each of us to have.[17] We don't get to experience all He has in store for us. Instead, we shrink back and allow our fears to dictate and destroy us;[18] Or like the horse and mule, we must be led by bit and bridle to get us to come to Him because we have no understanding.[19] Let's not be that way. In humility, we can trust God and ask to be united with Him in the plans He has for us. Then we can show up whole-heartedly with confidence in what He's calling us to do.

Ways to Foster Humility

It is good to check our hearts every so often for signs of pride in our lives. If self-importance and entitlement begin to crop up, Schaffner offers us the following helpful ways to eliminate it:

Develop an accurate understanding of our *strengths and weaknesses*.

Own our imperfections. When we do, we no longer waste our energy hiding them from others but can instead seek to learn to live with them productively or even to overcome them.

Get rid of a stubbornly low opinion of ourselves, as it contradicts humility. Extremely low self-esteem, just as a narcissistic overvaluation of our talents, lacks accuracy. It is just an inverted form of self-obsession, another way of fixating on ourselves rather than directing our attention toward others.

Although we are [subjects in our world, we must remember that we are objects in everybody else's]. We are not the center of the universe. This involves *adjusting our perspective*. Our woes and desires become ever more insignificant as we step away from them and consider the bigger picture. Our time on this planet is limited. Our works and achievements are transient.

We are all *parts of structures more significant than ourselves* – couples, families, communities, nations, the organizations we work for, and the human species. We should never forget the many teams we are a part of – small and large. Sometimes, it is better to privilege the needs of our groups over our individual desires.[20]

We all came from families that may have helped or hindered our humility levels. We can hold onto the good our caregivers taught us and unlearn ways they missed the mark.

My mother and father taught me to be humble; my mother was a learner. She was always open to learning from anyone and everyone. I love that she was this way. Kudos to her for modeling this for me in my life. My father was able to laugh at himself and his imperfections. He used to tell me not to take things so seriously. I'm still learning this, but I hope to get better at it day by day.

Another way to achieve humility is to get away and immerse yourself in nature. When I went to Alaska, I became quiet and small among the mountains and glaciers around me.

When we see trees that have lived longer than we have and oceans so vast you cannot see where they begin or end, it is humbling to be in the very presence of them.

Psalm 8:4-8, The Message Version says: I look up at your macro-skies, dark and enormous, your handmade sky jewelry, moon and stars mounted in their settings.

Then I look at my micro-self and wonder, why do you bother with us? Why take a second look our way?

Different Ways We Learn

One of the reasons I wanted to write this book was to encourage others and to help them understand and remember God's Words so they could refer to them in their time of need.

As a teacher, at the start of each school year I focused on getting to know my students, and how they best learned. They each had different learning styles, strengths/weaknesses, and career interests. The more ways I could identify their learning styles and include it in their coursework, taking account their strengths and weaknesses, and pairing it with their interests, the better the outcome of their school year would be.

In the same way, we can retain God's Words by using different learning methods, such as writing down scripture on index cards, taking bite sized phrases of scripture, and adding to them one by one, and repeating them out loud until they're committed to memory. Coloring pictures with a memory verse, solving verse crosswords, and hidden word finds aid both the visual and kinesthetic learner and helps to make learning God's Word more fun and engaging.

Moving our bodies to music with scripture or listening to an uplifting song adds another learning dimension. It acts as a one-two punch for memorizing key verses and comprehending them in physical expression.

Auditory learners may enjoy listening to the words of spiritual songs while singing out loud, and visual learners may benefit by seeing the terms of the lyrics written down. Music can be a powerful vehicle for learning. The more modalities used in memory work, the better.

Reading/Writing Learners can read spiritual books, take notes, and research words and scriptures to further their learning. (See Appendix 1)

Accepting your Assignment

As Christians, we are all part of Christ's body, but there are different parts within His body. Not all of us are ministry leaders, but we all can be ministers of God's Word in words or actions. Let me explain.

Several months before the woman's retreat, I eagerly paid for my spot at the event where my friend would be speaking at, my other friends would be going, too. It included a two-night, three-day stay at a lodge in the beautiful mountains of Pennsylvania in early fall, just as the leaves began turning their vibrant reds and oranges. As it turned out, I wasn't supposed to be there. Here's why.

After I signed up for the retreat, the school year began, and I received my schedule. Terror struck when I realized I'd be teaching two new subjects and had to work around the clock to make curriculum and lesson plans. I didn't have three hours to go on a retreat, never mind three days, so I canceled the trip.

"I hope you change your mind," my friend said when I told her I couldn't attend the weekend. She didn't understand. When you focus on your calling, you will find yourself saying "no" to many good things and only "yes" to a few.

As the Psalmist says, "Everything is permissible, but not everything is beneficial."

If we are to heed our calling in one area, we won't be able to do the things the crowd is doing. We must learn to prioritize and plan our lives, so they line up to what we're called to do.

I know of a person who wanted to be a minister in the Kingdom of God but is a much better businessperson. He can drum up business wherever he goes. With this gift, he can reach out to people, invite them to church events, and give generously to many people in need, and he is having a blast doing it. This is his gift, the work given to him by the Master Planner.

For me, God calls me to write. He also calls me to teach, but I can balance the two by writing in the summer and teaching the rest of the year. I fellowship with two amazing writing groups, one in Bergen County, NJ and another on Zoom with Christians from all over the globe who share a passion for acting and writing. These groups and the times we meet are precious to me. They encourage me. In these groups we do God's important work.

When I make my plans, I prioritize the most important things and try to keep a balance. First, I am a child of God. I make time for Him in the morning and throughout my day. He's my everything. Then, I am a wife to my husband. I make sure our needs are met, and that we are regularly connecting, and communicating. Then my children, that their schoolwork is done, dinner is on the table, we are doing things together. Then I make time to fellowship with other Christians, so we are mutually edified, and I look to meet needs for the lost world.

To avoid burnout, I take my Sabbath day each week, usually at sundown on Friday night until the following Saturday evening. During this time, I take care of myself and enjoy my family. We eat a shared take-out meal and I try not to do what I do during the rest of the week as much as possible. This way, I am eager to get back to it on Monday morning.

In this season of life, He's given me the work of educating special needs children. I also write. I take great pleasure in my writing. It's how I express myself best. To make time for my writing, I must say "no" to many good things to ensure I honor God with the essential work He's given me to do. Even when others might not get it.

Jesus's mother didn't understand what her Son's business was. It says in Luke 2:41-49 that when He was twelve years old, He stayed back after the Passover festival to listen to the religious teachers and ask them questions. When she and Joseph discovered Jesus was missing, they went back to get Him. When they found Him, she asked, "Son, why have you treated us like this?" He replied, "Didn't you know I must be in my Father's house?"[21] Jesus knew who He was and where He needed to be at that time.

Like Jesus, I needed to place limits on my activities. There was only so much I could accomplish in a week. So, when another event came up, and I got a text from my friend asking who's going, my response was, "I can't make it." It was best if I made progress on my writing goals.

Like the pine tree that doesn't try to be an Oak, we stay in our own lane. We don't overstep the boundary lines that have been given to us that have fallen in pleasant places.[22] We don't scratch and claw for positions, titles, and roles that are not ours to take. Instead, we encourage others in their work as we humbly and gratefully live out the role He has generously given us. And we shine brightly in those places.

When I called the woman from the retreat and told her I could not attend because a work obligation came up, without even asking, she gracefully gave me an unexpected full refund. This was a much-appreciated added blessing.

That is the power of God.

Questions

1. Pride usually shows up in my life in one of two ways; either I don't feel good enough (I'm not worthy, or I don't care about my needs, etc.) or arrogance (competing, comparing, feeling superior to others, entitled, deserving, etc.).
In what ways does pride show up in your life?

_____

_____

_____

_____

2. Dr. Schaffner offered some ways to foster humility. Which one(s) resonated with you most?

_____

_____

_____

_____

3. The four basic ways in which people learn are auditorily by listening, visually by seeing, kinesthetically by moving and by reading/writing. What kind of learner are you? What ways of memorizing scriptures appeal to you?

_____

_____

_____

_____

4. Are there things you are doing now that are permissible, but take time away from doing what is best for you? What steps will you take to rearrange your schedule to make room for what God is calling you to do?

_____

_____

_____

_____

Reflection

Matthes defines "humbling oneself" as not being "less than human," but coming ever closer, step by step, to the bliss and full flourishing for which we were made. What does this mean to you?

_____

_____

_____

_____

God's Promise

"Humble yourselves, therefore, under God's mighty hand, that he may lift you up in due time."

1 Peter 5:6

Jesus told His disciples to take the lowest seat at the table when they went to a dinner party. In doing so, they might be honored when the host comes and tells them to move up to a better seat.[23]

In what ways has God lifted you up when you humbled yourself?

_____

_____

_____

_____

Chapter Four - Verse Find
2 Corinthians 12:10

"That is why for Christ's sake, I delight in weaknesses, in insults, in hardships, in persecutions, in difficulties. For when I am weak, then I am strong."

```
M  T  Y  D  R  A  N  V  X  D  P  Z  W  C  E
W  W  W  E  A  K  N  E  S  S  E  S  E  W  V
R  F  R  H  H  R  W  I  Q  Z  R  T  A  J  R
G  Q  L  I  E  A  J  I  Z  I  S  R  K  K  I
I  A  U  E  Z  N  R  B  N  W  E  O  M  F  E
I  E  Q  R  D  U  I  D  P  S  C  N  A  C  S
Q  P  K  H  E  I  J  E  S  T  U  G  H  H  E
M  V  Q  D  V  N  O  L  W  H  T  L  B  R  N
G  Q  V  J  D  I  U  I  T  E  I  Z  T  I  C
V  C  S  J  G  R  S  G  X  N  O  P  S  S  P
W  P  T  R  A  J  S  H  B  U  N  D  S  T  P
Y  H  C  T  C  V  G  T  H  Z  S  J  O  S  J
E  J  J  C  G  W  D  V  Q  D  L  Q  R  W  D
D  I  F  F  I  C  U  L  T  I  E  S  J  T  P
T  Y  V  N  X  V  Q  P  E  W  M  Q  T  G  H
```

CHRISTS	WEAKNESSES	PERSECUTIONS	WEAK
SAKE	INSULTS	DIFFICULTIES	THEN
DELIGHT	HARDSHIPS	WHEN	STRONG

Chapter Five

The Word of God

"For the word of God is alive and powerful. It is sharper than the sharpest two-edged sword, cutting between soul and spirit, between joint and marrow. It exposes our innermost thoughts and desires."

Hebrews 4:12 (NLT)

I sat on my living room couch, trying to make sense of the many emotions swirling around in my mind: anger, fear, hopelessness. Mostly about my teaching job, but now it was my marriage. It was another day of my husband and I not looking each other in the eyes or connecting with each other emotionally. Instead, we passed by each other like two ships until we went to bed separately, at differing times of the night.

Everything felt like it was falling apart. The start of the new school year was the busiest one yet. My husband started his computer club which meant he had to get up and go to bed earlier than usual, and I felt like I was drowning in my weekly workload of writing curriculum and lesson planning. We hadn't had time for much else, even for one another. Finally,

I decided to talk openly to my husband about it. Sharing my feelings was always difficult to do. It was easier for me to stay bitter, critical and blame him for our lack of communication. But I was determined to change my ways.

"I'm struggling!" I called out to him in the kitchen where he was making a sandwich for tomorrow's lunch.

"We haven't connected in a while." I continued. "I think our priorities are not right. We need to make time for each other. We can't keep going on like this."

I waited in silence for his reply.

"It's the beginning of the school year. Things will begin to slow down. It will not always be this way." He said it as if he hadn't noticed anything was wrong.

So, I decided to let it go, went to bed, and again trusted God that He would work it out with our schedules. The next day after work, my husband sat down on the couch with me, and we lovingly caught up with each other.

Rather than blame one another for who was at fault, we used "I" statements to tell each other how we were feeling. We used "we" statements to ensure each other that we were on the same team. I felt seen and heard and so did he.

We continued to talk about how we were doing and how our days at school were going. We looked at each other. We weren't rushing. It was kind and compassionate. We talked for a good while. We reminded each other that we cared for and were committed to one another.

It was just what I needed to feel emotionally close to my husband again. *Phew. Thank you, God.*

When emotions are running high, it's best not to react in the moment. Open communication, a good night's sleep, and some time to think things through may be all that is needed to bring love and care back into a relationship.

Feelings

God has equipped us with many feelings: gladness, anger, embarrassment, sadness, and fear, to name a few. Feelings can be helpful indicators to let us know how things are going. When we are angry, our annoyance may be telling us a boundary line has been crossed, and we need to speak up. Or it may be us, and we need to get away and pray for patience. Sometimes we don't know why we're feeling a certain way. We must ask God to help us understand how we're feeling so we can respond to others responsibly. If we have no feelings at all, we ask God to give us a feeling heart, a heart of flesh.

When we feel contentment or joy, it prompts us to praise God and declare His goodness. When we feel hurt, our feelings tell us whether to confront a friend about a remark that didn't sit well. Feelings tell us when we are doing too much, and we need to cut things out of our schedules. When we feel ungrateful, or critical of others, they remind us we need to repent and be grateful and encouraging.

Sometimes our feelings lie to us. If they lead us to act contrary to the Bible's truth, we must train our minds to reject our faulty thinking.[1] We must teach our thoughts to be Godly, so they align with the Truth. For example, if I think negatively of myself or others, my feelings will follow and I become sad, angry, or hopeless. These feelings are felt because of a lie we believe. I know this because the Bible tells me in Psalm 139:14 that we are fearfully and wonderfully made.

However, if I realized I've committed a sin, I will feel bad about it and will want to make it right. But God never intended us to stay in this sorrowful state. Instead, He gave us a way out of those bad feelings. It's called repentance. He wanted us to change, move on and be free from guilt. There is no place for self-deprecation in God's plan for us. Jesus took care of that when He went to the cross.

 If we feel as if our gifts and talents are better than another person's, we must bathe our minds with the truth. We may have different strengths, and abilities than others, but to God we are all of equal value. Therefore, we remit these feelings as false, and with practice, our humility towards others will increase.

We are all sinners, beggars in God's sight, and dearly loved. Nobody is more valuable or valued than anyone else. The scriptures remind us we have all sinned and come short of the Glory of God.[2] It's by His grace we have been saved, through faith—not by our own doing but by the gift of God—not by our works, so that no one can boast.[3]

What Jesus did on the cross, we couldn't do for ourselves. We'll never be able to work our way into heaven, but we receive the gift of His righteousness by faith. This gift motivates us to say no to ungodliness. When we fall short, we repent and return to a right relationship with Him.

His love, mercy, and forgiveness is ours to receive if we believe it and claim it. When we do, we'll have a deep gratitude in our hearts that will overflow to others. When people ask us about the hope we have, we can share our faith with them. Perhaps they will make the decision to study the Bible, repent, be baptized and receive His forgiveness and grace, too.

God Breathed Words

While our words hold power, God's Words hold power and truth. With our words, we can build others up or tear them down. But when we store up His Words into our hearts, we can discern what is true and what is false. When others, or even ourselves accuse us, we can hold onto His words and let go of any lies. If others choose to gossip, or talk badly of us, we remember that our victory and honor come from God alone.[4] No longer do we need to get rattled by the opinions of others.

God spoke and the heavens came to be. He commanded, and the earth came into existence. He created life, and it stood firm.[5]

Scripture states that the words in the Bible were God breathed through the prophets as they were carried along by the Holy Spirit.[6]

The scriptures are alive, sharp, and effective. They train, correct, and rebuke us; they equip us for all the good work we will do.[7] They demolish the strongholds, lies, and mistruths we often cling to in our hearts and minds. They are life giving.

When we fill ourselves with Truth, it's like having a flashlight shine on our wrong thoughts, exposing them.[8] We fight the lies in our minds with the Words of Truth until our belief patterns begin to change.

If we feel hopeless, we hold onto those scriptures that restore us and remind us that He is our source of hope[9]. If we feel directionless, we remember His Words, "For I know the plans I have for you."[10] If we feel envious, jealous, or hateful towards another person, we look to the scriptures to help us with these wrong attitudes of the heart. They convict us of our error and help us find the strength to love and forgive.

Sometimes we must wrestle in prayer to love and forgive another person. When we choose the better response, we are blessed when we do. Since Jesus forgave us for the sins we've committed, how can we withhold our forgiveness from others?

The Word judges the thoughts and attitudes of our hearts and lays them bare before the One to whom we must give account.[11] Thank God I don't have to sit in insecurity, hatred, or annoyance towards others.

When we have self-control over our feelings, desires, and comforts and make them obedient to God's Words, and His purposes for us, we help ourselves and those around us. Just as when a kernel of wheat falls to the ground and dies and transforms into roots that go deep enough to reproduce itself, we, too, plant seeds of faith in others.[12] They go deep into the soul that at the right time God makes grow.

Thank you, Jesus; I can be quietly confident in your love and the plans you have for me and others. Thank you, Jesus, I can love others, and look at them with compassion, as your creations. I no longer desire to judge, criticize, or gossip about people because when I do, I am the one who stands condemned.

Stages of Life

Each of us are at different stages in life: we may be teens, singles, marrieds, marrieds with children, single moms and dads, widows, empty-nesters, or harvesters. The Scriptures give us instructions on how to live out each of these roles.

As a teacher, wife, mother, and homemaker, I must prioritize my day in the Word of God and listen to what He's saying to me. When I do I have a better chance at having the right attitude to serve my husband, children, students, and care for my home.

When I've had a terrible night's sleep and an emotionally draining day at work, I've learned the hard way that I need to take time for myself when I get home. I make sure I eat, nap, and pray so I'll have enough energy to finish out the rest of my day with a great heart.

Oftentimes, when I'm serving my family, I don't think about what I'm doing; I just do it. Matthew 6:3 says, "But when you give to the needy, do not let your left hand know what your right hand is doing."

Time for a Change

When I was single, before I became a Christian, I had given up on the religion with which my family raised me. My heart wasn't into it. I felt continuous guilt from the poor choices I often made, and the self-inflicted penance that followed. On the occasional holiday that I did attend church, my mind was elsewhere. I felt I was wasting my time. Deep down inside I knew there was a right way to live by God and I wasn't living it.

One day, a friend from work invited me to her church. Although I politely declined, our friendship grew over the weeks. When she asked me again, I accepted and went to a Sunday morning service. After service, I went to a Bible study. When my friend opened her Bible and showed me the scriptures about what the Bible said about Itself, I was amazed and wanted to learn more. Soon I became friends with people in different ministry groups. Marrieds, singles, campus, teens, and empty nesters. They all had Bibles and read them regularly. Each of them made the Bible their authority, and wholeheartedly applied what they were learning to their lives. Over the next nine days, I went to a few more studies. The next day, I was baptized. That was twenty-eight years ago.

The Word of God has given me freedom from not only my outward sins but the ones in my heart: my self-righteousness, criticalness, and judgmental attitude toward others. I studied how to change my way around, 180°. I realized I was a sinner, so I could be humble towards others, empathetic even. I grew in my encouragement toward people. I learned how God lavished His grace on me, especially when I messed up, and it helped me to extend the same grace to others.

Thank you, Jesus, that I can be myself. No longer must I live in slavery trying to attain perfection because only You were without sin before You took on ours. Thank you for Your gift of grace and let me be wholehearted in all I do because of what You've done for me. Let my sins always be before me lest I become self-righteous, again. Let me never take your love for granted, the love you showed me when you went to the cross for my sins. Thank you for the love you continue to show me as a big Brother who is by my side, who always guides me in the right way to go.

Tapping into the Power

God's Words hold power. No Word of God's will return empty, but He promises they will accomplish His purposes and desires.[13]

God's Words hold authority. When we store God's Words in our hearts, and They come into our minds in our time of need (or somebody else's), They accomplish what God intended. We may not know for what reason He will use them, but we trust that God does.

I listen to the Bible in a Year with Nicky Gumbel[14] most mornings on my way to work. The daily reading is about twenty minutes, the exact length of my commute. I love that it focuses on a scriptural topic in both the Old and New Testaments and relates them to real life. And both Testaments fit together. Listening to this everyday ensures I keep God's Words in my heart, and mind, so they are ready and available to retrieve in my time of need.

In the book of James, he tells us we must not merely listen to the Word of God but do what it says.[15] When I read a passage that tells me not to gossip, I believe this is my need for the day and I'm aware to steer clear of gossip.

When I have negative thoughts or am tempted to criticize, or complain, I usually return to Philippians 4:8, and try to think of what is true, noble, right, pure, lovely, admirable, excellent, or praiseworthy about the person or situation.

If I find myself participating in gossip or negative talk, it usually means I've forgotten my shortcomings and how much God has blessed me with, and I've become prideful and ungrateful.

If I have hatred in my heart toward somebody, then I've separated myself from the love of God. Instead, I aim to pray, love, serve, and be different. I want my light to shine brighter than ever, so He might be sought out and His name might be exalted by my actions.

Finally, because the Word of God works so powerfully in my life, I can't help but share it with others around me. Jesus said, "All authority in heaven and on earth has been given to me. Go therefore and make disciples of all nations, baptizing them in the name of the Father and of the Son and of the Holy Spirit, and teaching them to obey everything that I have commanded you."[16]

Sharing God's Words with others can be as simple as telling somebody what you learned in your quiet time, sitting down with somebody for a Bible Study, or imitating Jesus by doing what He did. Through all of these actions we help plant seeds in others while God makes things grow. Try reading the gospels (Matthew, Mark, Luke, and John) and see how Jesus interacted with others; it is fascinating. He's the Godman, and you will want to imitate Him. He knew what to do and say (and what not to) in every situation.

There is so much to learn from His example. There is so much hope and love to give to others.

Jesus is the Word of God

The Book of John starts with these words: "In the beginning was the Word, and the Word was with God, and the Word was God. He was with God in the beginning."

Scripture tells us Jesus is the Living Word of God, God's perfect revelation of Himself in the flesh. We can know God by learning from Jesus and how He lived while on the earth. He told one of His disciples, Philip, "Anyone who sees Me has seen the Father."[17] He says, "The Words I speak are Spirit and Life."[18] He not only is the personification of the Word of God, but He was with God in the beginning, and He has the Words of Eternal Life.[19]

Again, our words are powerful! We can use them to bring life, hope, and healing to others, or we can use them to bring death, harm, and to destroy each other. If we claim to have the Spirit in us yet justify using harsh words toward others, we must go back and read our Bibles! I've been the worst offender of this, but I am humbled and inspired by the following verses about the power of our words:

- "Life and death are in the power of the tongue."[20]
- "With the tongue, we praise our Lord and Father, and with it, we curse human beings, who have been made in God's likeness."[21]
- "Whenever you are arrested and brought to trial, do not worry beforehand about what to say. Just say whatever is given you at the time, for it is not you speaking, but the Holy Spirit."[22]
- "Therefore, I tell you, whatever you ask in prayer, believe that you have received it, and it will be yours."[23]
- "You brood of snakes! How could evil men like you speak what is good and right? For whatever is in your heart determines what you say."[24]
- "Knowing their thoughts, Jesus said, 'Why do you entertain evil thoughts in your hearts?'"[25]

We must be self-controlled and alert. We cannot let the devil get a foothold in our hearts.[26] Let's be people who store up good things inside of us so we can speak kind, powerful words of truth and encouragement to ourselves and others. Pray faithful words to God as we praise Him with gratitude for all He's given us.

The Gospel

There is nothing more powerful than raising someone from the dead, yet this is what God was able to do because Jesus trusted Him and the role His Father had for His Life. But there's more. When God raised Jesus back from the dead, He gave Him back His life for eternity. He gave Him all authority in heaven and on earth, and He was given back His relationship with God, His Father. And it gets even better. Because of Jesus's great love for His Father, and for us, He submitted to His Father's plan for His life. He gave us the same opportunity for eternal life with Him. And with the Father, too! Then, as an added bonus, He gave us freedom from sin, condemnation, and a powerful life if we decide to submit to the calling He has for us! This is good news!

Thank you, Jesus!

The Power of the Gospel

In Acts 9, Saul, later called Paul, was persecuting the Christians in the early church. Jesus got his attention one day by sending a bright flashing light from the sky, blinding him for three days, and directing him to go to Damascus to be told what he must do. When he got there, Ananias placed his hands on him, and his sight was restored. After this, he was converted, his mission being to preach the good news of Jesus.

Paul became so enthusiastic about spreading the gospel to others that he became *like* the people to win them over to God.[27] Paul was a changed man. The work he was now given to do by the Lord was based on what he was already gifted and talented at doing. Now instead of persecuting the Christians, he converted the people to Jesus!

I can't help but think that another reason God may have chosen him for this role was because he was given the gift of celibacy.[28] He was able to dedicate his entire life to preaching the gospel to everyone, first the Israelites then the Gentiles. In fact, he prayed that God would open a door for him[29] to preach this message because it was the reason he knew he was still on the earth.

Paul was so determined about his purpose that he adapted his behavior so he wouldn't offend weaker brothers who still followed the dietary laws of the Jewish customs. He said in 1 Corinthians 9:22, "To the weak, I became weak to win the weak," while remaining righteous to win others over to Christ. He said in 1 Corinthians 9:27, "I strike a blow to my body and make it my slave so that after I have preached to others, I myself will not be disqualified for the prize." Paul changed his ways and became relatable to others so not only would he win the prize, but others would, too.

Not everyone was like Paul. Another Christian in Acts 9:36 was a widow named Tabitha. She spent all her time doing good and helping the poor. When she died, Jesus enabled Peter to raise her back to life. Because of this miracle, many believed in the Lord.

In Acts 16:15 we learn of Lydia, a dealer in purple cloth. After her baptism, she practiced hospitality by inviting people to stay at her house.

When we seek God's Spirit for His direction and calling in our lives, we too will be wholehearted to participate in the role He's calling us heavenward to do. He will bring about the resources to make it happen.

Questions

1. Have you had any difficult feelings lately that indicate that something is not going right, or needs to change? If so, try to determine if these feelings are valid, or based on lies. How do you know?

_____

_____

_____

_____

2. The Word of God is powerful. It can demolish the strongholds in our lives. What scripture will you use to help you overcome a persistent sin, or a non-Truth you believe about yourself?

_____

_____

_____

_____

3. What does the Gospel mean to you? Why does Scripture say that it is the power of God?

_____

_____

_____

_____

Reflection

When we walk in the Spirit and yield to His control, we wait, watch, and listen for His promptings. When we allow Him to use us as vessels for His work, we live powerful lives. In what ways has the Spirit prompted you today?

_____

_____

_____

_____

God's Promise

"This day I call the heavens and the earth as witnesses against you that I have set before you, life and death, blessings, and curses. Now choose life so that you and your children may live and that you may love the LORD your God, listen to his voice, and hold fast to him."

Deuteronomy 30:19-20

Moses summoned the Israelites to make a choice whether to follow the Lord or not. He told them they'd receive life and blessings if they did, and death and curses if they didn't.

Why do you think Moses gave them a choice? Why do you think God gives us one?

_____

_____

_____

_____

We take captive
every thought
to make it
obedient
to Christ.
2 Corinthians 10:5

Chapter Six

Prayer

"Father, if you are willing, remove this cup from me.
Nevertheless, not my will, but yours, be done."

Luke 22:42

Last night I had a disagreement with my husband. This time it was about our son and a decision we had to make about his college prospects. Our conversation got so heated that I had to retreat to another room to de-escalate. I was angry and I knew if I continued to talk, nothing helpful was going to come out of my mouth. While in our separate spaces, I prayed to God. I told Him how upset I was and why I felt the way I did. As I heard myself, I began to see the sorrowful state I was in: the pride, fear, and lack of trust I had in my heart. It was then I decided to humble myself and express how I felt to my husband, once again, using "I" statements, i.e., (I felt bad because..., when you said this it made me feel...).

My husband is an awesome, godly man and very empathetic. When I didn't judge him for anything but simply told him how I felt about my wants and fears for our son, he was able to hear and respond to me. Putting myself in this vulnerable state allowed him to put down his defenses. Then he even shared how he felt. He made known to me his worries and fears, and we were able to relate and understand one another, and come to a better decision.

I love my husband. I remember we are one in Christ, and I'm committed to him. We've had our ups and downs in our twenty-five years of marriage. I'm convinced that God's power, His mercy, and our meager efforts to apply His Word to our relationship are the glue that continues to hold us together all these years.

But what if I had acted out in my anger and accused him of wrongdoing? What if I was not careful with my words and I expressed whatever came to mind? Unfortunately, early on in our marriage there were many times when I did this. I said a lot of things I regretted. Hurtful words are hard to "unsay."

When we learn to pause, hold our tongue, and go to God first in prayer, we can diffuse our high emotions. We can hold onto scriptures that remind us of the Truth. One good Scripture for this is, "Be not quick in your spirit to become angry, for anger lodges in the heart of fools."[1]

Meditation: The Gateway to Effective Prayer

What does meditation have to do with prayer?

When I think of meditation classes I've taken in the past, images of sitting on a yoga mat with legs crisscrossed and palms facing up on my knees come to mind. When the instructor tells the class to empty our minds, it feels like an act of futility as the thoughts of the day's events fight for our attention. But according to Dr. Tracy Jones, a Christian Meditation Instructor, this is not the way we should approach prayer.

Jones states, "Unlike Eastern meditation, where there is an emptying of the mind, Christian meditation calls us to fill the mind with God's Words and think of them throughout the day."[2] Meditation is an act by which we move the scriptures from our brains to our hearts so that we can use them in our time of need.

When I meditate on the Scripture, "God is love,"[3] I'm less likely to have unloving thoughts toward my husband, or anybody else, for that matter. When temptation strikes, I pray, *Lord, help me to love this person as you would.*

Then I imagine myself as I am, a sinner who struggles with pride and judgment in her heart. And it changes my attitude toward the person. I no longer see them in the same light. Instead, I see them as better than me because my sin is the worst. Remarkably, God has mercy on me when I'm in this humble state. He gives me grace upon grace, even when I feel I don't deserve it. However, I claim it nonetheless, lest God's grace be poured out to me in vain.

Teach Us How to Pray

How would you begin to talk to someone who was all-powerful, all-knowing, all-good, and everywhere simultaneously? Hopefully with humility, but Jesus gave His disciples a prayer model[4] to follow, and we can use it, too.

First, Jesus reminds us of the reverence we should have for God. He is in Heaven, and we're not. We are His creation. He is not ours. He doesn't need anything; we have many needs. His righteous ones are poor in spirit, and He listens to us when we come to Him in humility.

Next, we must remember that we can trust Him with our lives. Not only does He know the plans He has for us, but He has the best ones. So instead of seeking first what we want, we ask His will for our lives. He is faithful and will show us as we go. We may think we want one thing, but we often can't see the bigger picture of the good He's orchestrating for everyone.

Then, we ask Him for our daily bread, what we need to get through our day. When we ask and believe He will provide, we have no worries about tomorrow, nor do we dwell on the past. Instead, we put our trust in Him to meet our needs today.

We confess our sins, because our sin not only hurts us but those who are affected by our actions. We ask for His help to change us so we can be effective, protected, and forgiven. We thank Him for His grace when we mess up again. When others hurt us, we forgive them because He has forgiven us.

Finally, we thank Him for protecting us from Satan and the powers of darkness. We remember we are in a spiritual battle. We ask Him to keep us from sin's temptation. When we fall, we rely on the victory of Jesus because He's already won the battle for us.[5] We get up again because we must finish the race. Even when we fail, He still has plans for us, and will help us achieve all that He has for us to do.

When we pray with God and with others, our words need not be showy, just genuine, pure, and with faith. Even faith as small as a mustard seed will do.

The apostle Paul tells us we are to pray with all kinds of petitions, and requests, and with thanksgiving to God.[6] He also tells us to do it while rejoicing[7] (laughing, dancing, and having fun). *Wow!* It may be inappropriate to laugh, dance and have fun in the middle of a business meeting, but we can still do it in our hearts. *That's a sure way to get rid of anxiety. Try it.*

One of my favorite ways to pray is like King David in the Psalms. When writing this book, I attempted to imitate him by starting each chapter with a troubled heart. David began a Psalm with a heart filled with anxiety. But by the Psalm's end, he had regained his faith, held onto to God's Words, and claimed their promises. In this way, he achieved victory after victory in his battles.

David relied on God as if his life depended on it because it did. King Saul was after his life and throne, but David refused to give up on the plans the Lord had for him. The Psalms were written for us so we, too, could learn how to pray and rely on God. In them, David poured his heart out with every gut-wrenching feeling to the One who saw him, heard him, and could help him. He was considered a man after God's heart[8] because he was committed to doing things God's way despite how he felt.

When we pray and acknowledge our need for God's help in our lives: confessing our shortfalls, praising Him, thanking Him and presenting our requests to Him, we can be sure He hears us and is at work in our lives. He is our loving Father and creator in whom we can put our complete trust.

My Will Versus God's

There is great power in the person who empties himself and submits to God's will for their life. We've heard of the person who refuses to surrender to God. They are like a brute beast who needs to be muzzled by bit and bridle. They are disciplined by consequences, the law, or the system lest they change their ways. Because of their choices, there is little peace in their lives.

Not so those of us who are submitted to God. We are instruments, powerful vessels that a loving God can use. With us who are willing, no one can fathom what He will do with our lives when He is at the helm.

When we let go of our wants and desires and align them with God's, we may suddenly feel as if we are in a difficult situation. We may feel stuck, even. We are not used to stepping out in blind faith with Him to what He is calling us to do. We may prolong our time in this state of misery if we hesitate and continue battling on our own, apart from His will, but glory day when we finally take that leap of surrender. Not only will He give us the strength and courage to persevere, but He will guide us along the way. He will set up the meeting times and places with the people who can help. When we put our trust in Him with our calling and act in faith, He will open doors to dreams we didn't know were possible. He will fulfill longings deep in our souls that were previously beyond our comprehension.

If you feel you've hit a dead end in your plans, don't worry. God's plans are still in place. It's possible you're in a period of growing, pruning, or a season of waiting. Learning to persevere and seek His will takes time. My hope is we will day by day mature and grow into who we are to be, and what we are to do. As we go, we will share in His pleasure, and reap the rewards. He will fulfill the plans He purposed for us.

Wrestling in Prayer

When Jesus was in the Garden of Gethsemane, He pleaded with His Father to take the cup of suffering away from Him. He didn't want to die on the cross. Even after wrestling in prayer that night, His Father didn't take it away. He knew His anguish would last only a little while, and He gave Him the strength to endure it. His suffering seemed horrible in the moment, but later we would learn it was His sacrifice that gives us the opportunity to be in a right relationship with His Father.

When we plead with God to take away a challenging situation, and it doesn't happen, it may be His will that we go through it because of the greater good it will produce. If so, He'll be with us, giving us the strength to endure.

Faith

There are many great ways to build faith. One way is by reading the Bible regularly. Power comes when we apply what we've learned to our lives. Faith grows when we believe the promises He has for our lives and act as if we do, too. Especially when we fall short and must rely on His grace.

Going to church builds my faith. These days I go to church in person or on Zoom. Sometimes the message coincides with what I'm learning in my quiet times. When this happens, my faith grows. Or I'll connect with someone struggling with the same thing as I am. We'll pray for each other to overcome our challenges, and our faith continues to grow. When I encounter new believers who just came from their empty way of life, or when I talk to seasoned believers who know how to gently guide me to truth and grace, my faith grows even more. Together, we fellowship and build each other up as we help one another remain faithful. Just as the scripture says, "As iron sharpens iron, so one man sharpens another."[9]

The Holy Spirit

One of our greatest gifts we receive when we become Christians is The Holy Spirit, who lives inside us. The power of the Holy Spirit advocates for and reminds us of everything Jesus said in the Bible. Have you ever had a Scripture pop into your mind when you needed it? That's the work of the Holy Spirit reminding us of Truth.

Having the Holy Spirit is a tremendous privilege but also a huge responsibility. If we allow negative thoughts to overtake our hearts and minds or believe things contrary to what the scriptures tell us, we grieve the Spirit[10], and He no longer is helpful to us.

But if we live according to the Spirit, not gratifying the sinful nature, we attune ourselves to Him, and He guides us.[11] We want Him with us because we need His help.

Praying the Scriptures with Faith

Did you ever catch yourself praying from a heart filled with fear and doubt? At one time I felt the Lord was too busy to take time from His schedule to listen to me. I thought my life wasn't valuable enough for Him to go out of His way to "bother" with me. When I took this posture, I had a powerless prayer life because I didn't claim what the scriptures said.

As Christians, we are in God's favor. We're on the inside, and He no longer holds our sins against us. We still confess them, but He's forgiven them: past, present, and future. He's not the judge who condemns us. Nor does He have any animosity toward us. We are His children on whom He wants to lavish all His promises. We are His children in whom He delights.[12]

When I ponder God's Words and allow them to permeate my mind, they come back to me in my time of need. They correct my skewed thoughts and give me comfort and strength throughout my day.

When fears, doubts, and worries try to push their way into my heart and mind, the following scriptures proclaimed in prayer help me to remember the Truth.

- Lord, the fear of man no longer has a hold on me. My honor and victory come from you, alone. Only you are to be feared. You say that perfect love drives out fear, that there is no fear in love.[13] Thank you for Your perfect love for me so that I, too, can love others in every situation.

- Lord, you give me everything good that I have: my husband, my children, their futures, my relationships, the work of my hands, my ability to write, my creativity, and all the plans you have for me. All these are yours that you entrusted to my care. I trust you will guide me in all your ways. Give me strength and wisdom so you can fulfill the plans you have for my life.

- Lord, you tell me not to worry about anything but to pray about everything.[14] You know my anxious thoughts. Thank you for taking care of tomorrow and being with all the details of the day. I prepared the best I could. Help me enjoy the day and live in the moment that I might make the most of it by being attentive to others' needs. Help me listen to others, to know when to speak and when to refrain.

- Lord, it is not my job to fix people. Help me accept how you created others. I trust You are working in their lives. Guide me in all my conversations. Help them to be full of grace and seasoned with salt so I may know how to answer everyone.[15]

- Lord, I am free to be joyful because I trust you with the plans you have for my life, my loved ones, and the lives of those around me. Help me be still and know that you are God.[16] You are working even when I don't see it. Help me to cast all my anxiety on you because you care about me. [17]

- Lord, thank you that because of the death, burial, and resurrection of Jesus, I can have peace and confidence forever.[18] I no longer need to work to prove myself worthy of your love. Instead, I can rest, trusting in what Jesus did on the cross. I need not fear man's judgment or condemnation. You are my maker and helper. What can man do to me?[19] Help me, Lord, overcome my fear of man. You alone are my Lord.

- Help me claim your promises as you make them known to me. Help me repent of my fearful and faithless ways. Because you continually love and forgive me, I can continually love and forgive others.

Questions

1. What do you think of when you think of meditation? How does filling your mind with God's Words help you throughout your day?

_____

_____

_____

_____

2. Jesus wrestled in prayer in the Garden of Gethsemane. He didn't want to suffer an excruciating painful, and shameful death on a cross. Nor did He want to be forsaken by God when He took on all the sins of the world. Yet God wouldn't take it away from Him. Why do you think God wouldn't take it away from Him? Why do you think He was able to go through with it?

_____

_____

_____

_____

3. James 5: 13 says, "Is anyone among you in trouble? Let them pray. Is anyone happy? Let them sing songs of praise." Which of James's statements apply more to you right now? Why not pray and sing praises by writing

them down in the space below.

_____

_____

_____

_____

Reflection

Thessalonians 5:16-18 tells us to be joyful always, pray continuously, and be thankful in all situations. God wants us to be positive, satisfied, optimistic, prayerful, and grateful.

What does this remind us to do when we are having a bad day, feeling depressed, or having a complaining attitude?

Go back to Chapter One of this book and re-read the section on Who You Are in Christ. As you do, write down prayers of thankfulness for who He says you are until your joy overflows.

_____

_____

_____

_____

God's Promise

"Therefore, confess your sins to each other and pray for each other so that you may be healed. The prayer of a righteous person is powerful and effective."

James 5:16

Confessing our sins is a command from God. What do prayer, righteousness, and healing have to do with one another in this Scripture?

_____

_____

_____

_____

Chapter Six - Crossword Puzzle
Directions: Use the Clues Below to Complete the Crossword Puzzle that Contain the Words in Philippians 4:5-7

"Let your gentleness be evident to all. The Lord is near. Do not be anxious about anything, but in every situation, by prayer and petition, with thanksgiving, present your requests to God. And the peace of God, which transcends all understanding, will guard your hearts and your minds in Christ Jesus."

Across	Down
3. Bring before (God)	**1.** Watch over with great care
5. The faculty of consciousness and thought	**2.** Outside of the human ability to grasp or perceive
6. A short distance away	**4.** Making a request
7. Rest in a right relationship with God	**8.** Easily seen or understood, obvious
11. Calm, kind, or careful understanding	**9.** To express the desire for
12. Expression of gratitude	**10.** The seat of life or strength, one's emotional nature
13. The result of uncertainty	

Chapter Six - Crossword Puzzle

peace

Part 3

The Peace

What minor irritations or day-to-day mishaps do you let steal your joy and upset your peace of mind? Was it the recycling container that blew down the street, leaving bottles, wrappings, and paper all over the front yard? Or was it the classmate or co-worker who continued to push all your buttons? Are you worried about money? How you'll pay for college, make a living, buy a home, or retire one day?

Whatever causes a lack of peace in our lives must be brought to the foot of the cross and surrendered. We cannot allow our troubles to dictate our joy levels. Dwelling over the past or worrying about the future does not cultivate in us a joyful heart. We must choose to let it go, trust God, and seek His guidance for making the next right move going forward.

A perfect life is an illusion. We need to expect trouble and learn from the Prince of Peace who has shown us the way to live and overcome the world.

Thought Questions

1. What does it mean to have God's favor? What is the Gospel of Peace?

2. How can you be steadfast in your mind? How does a mind fixed on Jesus produce peace?

3. What are the standards of the world vs. the standards of God? How do we live in the world without conforming to its ways?

Chapter Seven

In God's Favor

"Therefore, since we have been made right in God's sight by faith, we have peace with God because of what Jesus Christ our Lord has done for us."

Romans 5:9-10 (NLT)

I called my twenty-four-year-old son the other day. He was driving to a job site for one of his businesses.

"Is this a good time?" I asked him.

"Yeah, it's perfect." He said enthusiastically. "I just got in my car and have a 30-minute drive."

"Great! How's it going?" I continued.

He began, "My business partner just got baptized."

"What?" I asked him. "How did that happen?"

"He asked me to smoke weed with him, and I told him I didn't do that because I was a Christian." He continued, "He studied the Bible with me and Pablo, another brother from church. A few days later, Pablo had the faith he could become a Christian. His friend continued studying the scriptures, and a week later, they baptized him in the Pacific Ocean."

I stood there listening to him on the phone in utter amazement. Not only because this person became a Christian, but because Zach's friend worked at a high-end automobile dealership and was rich.

Because of their common interests, He and Zach became fast friends, and soon went into business together, flipping cars. They bought quality cars at a low price and sold them quickly for a profit. In my limited understanding, I believed people who owned fancy cars and pursued wealth had no interest in God. Didn't Jesus tell His disciples it was impossible when He spoke to them about the rich young ruler?[1]

But I was wrong. Jesus did not say it was impossible. He said it was hard. Why? Because money does that to people. Big money has the purchasing power to grant us almost anything our hearts' desire, everything except the most important thing, a relationship with God. And God is a jealous God who tells us we can't serve two masters.[2]

When people see our faith and convictions about staying away from drugs, being good stewards of our money, and living within our means, others are empowered to want to do the same. They, too, believe they can be free from the enslavement of drugs, the love of money, and the desire for more possessions. When we free ourselves from these things, we can worship God alone, and He will meet our daily needs.

When we have the privilege of bringing another believer to Christ, there is a party in heaven.[3] As we use our gifts to serve Him and others, He is glorified, and others will praise His name. When we've been faithful with the little things He's given us, He will say, "Well done, good and faithful servant. I'll entrust you with some more.[4]"

We can honor and serve God in many ways: when we bring others to faith, strengthen the weak, encourage the oppressed, defend the fatherless, and plead the case of the widow,[5] among others.

A Right Relationship with God

While studying the Bible before I became a Christian, I learned what Jesus did on the cross for me, and I was baptized into Christ. I was a new creation and gained back my relationship with God.

In my Bible studies, I learned what was not pleasing to God: lying, gossiping, getting drunk, and I repented of many of my outward sins. They were obvious.

But my heart sins were another story. Some of these were not even apparent to me, and I had to have someone else point them out. Even now, I struggle daily with them. But this does not mean God has turned His back on me. No. I still have His favor because I acknowledge my sin, repent of it, and move on. I know Jesus's blood has atoned for them, past, present, and future.

Remaining in Christ

Jesus said, "Remain in me, and I will remain in you. A branch cannot produce fruit if it is severed from the vine, and you cannot be fruitful unless you remain in me."[6]

When we remain in Him, He says He will produce fruit in our lives. Our goal is to nurture our relationship with Him.

We build our relationship with Jesus by spending time with Him, talking and listening to Him in prayer, reading the Word of God, applying what we're learning to our lives, and talking to others about it as we go. When I've had a great quiet time in the morning, it changes the way I act and speak at work. Instead of spreading negativity or participating in gossip, I'll speak what's positive and true. I will naturally tell my friends, and family what I'm learning as I go about my day.

Remaining in Christ also means trusting and believing what Jesus says is true and holding onto it as if our life depended on it, because it does.

Fruits of the Spirit

The fruits of the Spirit are the mark of Christian character. Who wouldn't want them? Love, joy, peace, patience, kindness, goodness, faithfulness, gentleness, and self-control.[7] Many of us miss receiving them because we are trying to achieve them on our own strength. Instead, we must trust His guidance, and follow the path to where He's directing us. We must get rid of our insecurity, stop looking at what others are doing and believe God's got the perfect plan for our lives. We will forge ahead on the path marked out for us and will be in perfect peace when we do.[8] Sure, the ride may get bumpy, but He is with us and will see us through.

Stages in Our Relationship

As Christians, we go through various stages in our relationship with God. In the beginning, I compare it to a child who is adored by his earthly father. This child of his is free to explore the world, fall, pick himself back up, and keep going. Occasionally, he tests his boundaries and gets a little "no, no, no" and a finger shaken at him when he goes beyond them.

Later in the relationship, it's like spending time with your best friend. He knows you inside and out, is with you through good times and bad, and wants nothing more than to support you, not harm you and be by your side as you prosper in life together.

Finally, it's like your lover, who you are wild about. You want nothing more than to be with him, please him, and tell him your thoughts and desires. You can't wait to discover new things together. The time spent with him fuels the rest of your activities. When others see your radiance and passion, you tell them all about him.

With God

Our greatest source of peace is knowing we are in a right relationship with God. Once we establish that, we can come to Him on a different level. While I believe our relationship with God grows deeper over time, some of us may be stuck relating to Him in a way other than what He intended.

In the book, With, by Skye Jethani, he writes about the four different postures humans may take as they relate to God. They are *Life under God, Life over God, Life from God, and Life for God*, each of these stemming from man's fear and desire for control.

Life under God seeks to control the world by securing God's blessing via rituals and/or morality. What better way to control the world than by controlling the God who created it? *Life over God* takes a slightly different approach. It employs natural laws or divine principles (taken) from the Bible to help us through life's challenges. Want to avoid catastrophe? Then organize your life around God's principles. *Life from God* is primarily concerned with scarcity-not having enough. Amass enough wealth, health, and popularity and you can insulate yourself from the calamities that befall others. And all of these commodities are best acquired *from* God. *Life for God* as depicted by the older son in Jesus' parable, tries to extract God's favor through faithful service. Accomplish enough for God and he will bless and protect you.

(When we) attempt to control the world in order to alleviate our fears-especially our fear of death-it is never enough.

Real faith, real surrender is *only* possible in the *Life with God* posture. As John said, "Perfect love casts out fear." We live with God when we are united with him and experience his goodness and love, fear loses its grip on our souls. With promises of God's boundless love, *Life with God* breaks endless cycles of fear and striving for control. [9]

Isaiah 43:1b-2 says, "Do not fear, for I have redeemed you; I have summoned you by name; you are mine. When you pass through the waters, I will be with you; and when you pass through the rivers, they will not sweep over you. When you walk through the fire, you will not be burned.; the flames will not set you ablaze."

Our relationship with God in this world doesn't promise an easy life without troubles. But when we go through difficult times, He promises He will be right there with us.[10]

Thank you, God.

Questions

1. We can honor and serve God in many ways: when we bring others to faith, strengthen the weak, encourage the oppressed, defend the fatherless, and plead the case of the widow, among many others. Brainstorm some different ways you can use your talents and gifts to serve Him and others. When we do, we please Him and bring Him glory. What ways did you come up with to serve Him, and others?

_____

_____

_____

_____

2. What does it mean to be in a right relationship with God? What does it mean to remain in Him?

———————————————————————————————————

———————————————————————————————————

———————————————————————————————————

———————————————————————————————————

3. Which of the five postures from Skye Jethani's book, *With*, do you find yourself relating to God most often? If it's not in the "with" posture, how will you begin changing the way you relate to Him?

———————————————————————————————————

———————————————————————————————————

———————————————————————————————————

———————————————————————————————————

Reflection

God wants a relationship with us. He wants us to be sorrowful and repentant of our sin when we see it. Sin separates us from God, and hurts ourselves, and others. This should make us earnest and eager to change it. He doesn't want us to sit in guilt, nor condemnation. Before Jesus "died" on the cross, He stated, "It is finished."[11] And at that moment, "the temple curtain was torn in two from top to bottom. The earth shook, the rocks split, and the tombs broke open."[12]

A "Day of Atonement" is no longer needed each year when the high priest sacrificed animals to cover the people's sins and guilt. The tearing of the curtain represented the new way we are to have a relationship with God because of Christ's sacrifice for our sins.

For those of us who believe, Christ's sacrifice was the gateway to a relationship with God and peace in our hearts (not guilt) for those who continue in Him. What does this mean to you?

———————————————————————————————————

———————————————————————————————————

———————————————————————————————————

———————————————————————————————————

God's Promise

"Therefore, since we have been justified through faith, we have peace with God through our Lord Jesus Christ, through whom we have gained access by faith into this grace in which we now stand."

Romans 5:1-2

As Christians, we can fear and doubt where we stand with God and often feel insecure in our relationships with other believers. How would your interactions with God and other Christians be if you believed and functioned as if you had God's favor because of what Christ did for you?

_____

_____

_____

_____

Chapter Seven - Verse Find
Isaiah 43:1

*"Do not fear for I have redeemed you; I have summoned
you by name; you are mine."*

```
V  O  S  J  Q  M  I  K  U  V  X  Y  R  S  Z
Z  G  S  G  Q  S  W  Y  G  M  J  H  E  U  K
V  F  K  N  K  H  D  U  A  O  H  T  D  Z  Q
S  X  E  M  V  E  T  J  C  E  Y  S  E  N  T
X  H  G  A  I  I  R  X  O  P  L  J  E  O  L
V  F  F  D  Y  N  A  M  E  W  T  F  M  F  J
H  N  D  B  B  T  E  R  H  B  L  U  E  W  N
G  N  U  O  Z  C  B  F  E  A  R  B  D  D  M
V  H  S  X  D  W  A  A  Y  Y  V  W  T  N  S
X  Z  M  F  Q  S  U  M  M  O  N  E  D  V  V
O  Z  O  R  X  P  S  L  P  U  U  N  O  T  Z
T  R  E  C  B  Y  W  L  G  K  D  Y  W  A  L
Y  C  Z  O  P  U  B  T  M  G  F  O  M  G  P
V  H  L  L  K  A  C  C  J  P  B  N  G  V  M
X  Y  N  O  Q  O  Y  B  D  Q  N  G  H  L  Y
```

DO	REDEEMED	SUMMONED	YOU
NOT	YOU	BY	ARE
FEAR	HAVE	NAME	MINE

Chapter Eight

Keep Going

"You will keep in perfect peace him whose mind is steadfast because he trusts in you."

Isaiah 26:3

I turned the corner and headed up the road on my early morning jog. I was near the spot where I had taken that terrible fall three weeks before when suddenly I was struck with terror. *What if I go back there and fall again, or what if something worse happens?*

I carefully avoided the area but felt prompted to turn around and return to where I had fallen. I wanted to face my fear head-on. While still jogging in place, I made a U-turn in the middle of the road and headed toward that dreadful spot where I had broken my ankle.

My heart began beating hard and fast. I stopped, peered through the fence, and carefully, oh, so carefully tip toed over the sidewalk into the grassy area that separated the sidewalk from the road and noticed it was uneven. *I'd better watch out for those bumpy surfaces,* and off I went to finish my morning run.

Fear of the Unknown

We will face many fears in life: some real and some imaginary. When we are in a fight or flight situation, the body produces stress hormones causing the heart to pump blood into the limbs to get us ready for action. However, there is another type of response we can have, like the fight or flight one, but there is no real danger. It exists only in our minds. They occur due to genetics, stress, or significant life changes.

Last August, I began worrying about what assignment I would teach for the upcoming school year. Working in Special Education, I usually don't hear where I'll be placed until just before the first days of school. This particular year was no exception.

However, the reaction I had this year was different, more significant. As each day passed without hearing a word about my schedule, I became increasingly anxious and fearful. I told my husband about my struggle. He sat down with me, and we made a plan that I would contact my supervisor. The next day I had a video conference with my department head, and she did let me know where I'd be teaching. *Easy enough.*

But come September, my schedule changed. Instead of the study skills class I was used to teaching, I was given two new classes, both for which I had to develop new curriculum and lesson plans. It was a program new to the district, and I didn't have much support. My part-time hours became full-time as my work suddenly took over my weekends, and evenings. Just to keep up with my workload, I declined invitations, social events, and even cancelled a weekend trip with my girlfriends. I felt like I was drowning in a never-ending cycle of curriculum writing and lesson planning.

Late one night in my bed, my heart began beating loudly, as if it was pounding out of my chest. Then it stopped. Then it pounded again. I thought I was dying. This continued until I sat on the edge of my bed and called out to my husband, "I think I need to go to the emergency room. I think my heart stopped beating."

Looking back, it seemed laughable. But if you've never had a panic attack, this is what it felt like. Thankfully, my husband talked me through it. We never ended up going to the ER, but I was beginning to understand the impact of how stress affects the body.

Obstacles

I'm a visionary, dreamer, and planner. I love to make goals and achieve them. Usually, if I set out to do something, I will finish it. Not everyone is like this. My husband is the opposite. He likes to take one day at a time and see how things go. It used to drive me crazy. But I've learned to appreciate his way of planning things. Even though I still like to plan my work and work my plan, he helps me to be flexible along the way.

God knows I want to publish this book one day and have others resonate with its message. I also hope to open an on-line shop where I will sell inspiring merchandise, t-shirts, stationery, and stickers. But I'm not ready to give up my teaching gig just yet. And we need the extra income. I need to set some boundaries at work and not let things get to me. Let's wait and see what the next school year brings. I think God has more in store for me in learning to trust in His timing.

When obstacles stand in the way of our goals, we mustn't give up on them. When God told Moses He was giving the land of Canaan to His people, most of the Israelites backed out. Why? They feared the "giants" in the land and didn't trust God's perfect plan.

In Numbers 13:1-2, the Lord told Moses to send some men to explore the land of Canaan, which He was going to give to the Israelites. But before He gave it to them, there were some things they had to do first.

He told Moses to send one leader from the twelve ancestral tribes to the land. He told them to see what it was like, whether the people there were strong or weak, few or many; whether the land was good or bad, and if somebody reinforced the walls for an attack, if the soil was poor or fertile, and to bring back some of the fruit that was there.[1]

Why did He tell them this? Why didn't God just give it to them without having them assess it first?

After exploring the land for forty days, they returned to Moses and Aaron and reported what they saw. They responded, "We went into the land to which you sent us, and it does flow with milk and honey! Here is its fruit. But the people who live there are powerful, and the cities are fortified and very large."[2]

Do you sense some fear and doubt here? Do the obstacles in your life make you fear and doubt what God is calling you to do? What do you do when things seem impossible?

"Then Caleb [one of the twelve from the tribe of Judah] silenced the people before Moses and said, "We should go up and take possession of the land, for we can certainly do it.""[3]

Thank goodness, somebody was faithful!

"But the men who had gone up with him said, "We can't attack those people; they are stronger than we are." And they spread a bad report about the land they had explored among the Israelites. They said, "The land we explored devours those living in it. All the people we saw there are of great size. We saw the Nephilim there (the descendants of Anak). We seemed like grasshoppers in our own eyes, and we looked the same to them.""[4]

Oh No! They are giving way to fear. They have lost their faith! They are giving way to their perceived obstacles instead of trusting what God had promised them. Even worse, they spread their faithlessness to the rest of their community! Then they started complaining!

All the community members raised their voices and wept aloud that night. All the Israelites grumbled against Moses and Aaron, and the assembly said, "If only we had died in Egypt! Or in this wilderness! Why is the Lord bringing us to this land only to let us fall by the sword? Our wives and children will be taken as plunder. Wouldn't it be better for us to go back to Egypt?' And they said to each other, 'We should choose a leader and go back to Egypt.'[5]

Then Moses and Aaron fell face down in front of the whole Israelite assembly gathered there. Joshua the son of Nun and Caleb the son of Jephunneh, who were among those who had explored the land tore their clothes and said to the entire Israelite assembly, "The land we passed through and explored is exceedingly good. If the Lord is pleased with us, He will lead us into that land flowing with milk and honey and give it to us. Only do not rebel against the Lord. And do not be afraid of the people of the land, because we will devour them. Their protection is gone, but the Lord is with us. Do not be afraid of them."[6]

Thankfully, Caleb had a faithful friend, Joshua. He didn't cave into fear because of what he saw or heard. Instead, he and Caleb believed what God promised.

But the whole assembly talked about stoning them. Then the glory of the Lord appeared at the Tent of Meeting to all the Israelites. The Lord asked Moses, "How long will these people treat me with contempt? How long will they refuse to believe in me, despite all the signs I have performed among them? I will strike them down with a plague and destroy them, but I will make you a nation greater and stronger than they."[7]

Then God struck down all the tribe leaders except Caleb and Joshua because they made the whole community grumble against Moses by spreading a bad word about the land God promised to give them.[8]

Reading these passages of Scripture was sobering and humbling. How often had I read that God promised to prosper and not harm me, yet I allowed obstacles and faithlessness get in the way? How often had I grumbled and complained about my friendships, work situations, marriage, children, and anything else God had graciously given me? How many times had He wanted to provide me with the promise of peace, but I refused to trust or be grateful for what I had?

When Moses reported to the Israelites all that had happened, it says the Israelites mourned bitterly. [9]

I must ask this question, if God says He will give us something, would we rather believe, and persevere through our fear? Or be afraid, give up, miss out, regret it, mourn over it and be bitter? *Hmm.*

What if instead, we could be like Caleb and Joshua and report to others about all the good that God has planned to give us since He has given us so much already?

If it is difficult for you to count your blessings, start with being thankful for shelter, clothes, and food. Then think about all He has given you because you are in Christ. If there is a particular promise that is difficult for you to believe, pray as if you've received it, then claim it daily for yourself. It is impossible for God to lie.

Whenever I choose to complain in my heart, or grumble to others, it's like spreading faithlessness to anyone with listening ears. What if instead, I decided to believe what God has already given me is good, and shared my gratitude about it with others?

Perhaps God told Moses to send the twelve leaders to check out the promised land so we would learn how to overcome our obstacles and trust

God with what He's already given us, too.

We would see all that God planned to give us: a land flowing with milk and honey, with fertile soil to grow trees that bear fruit to eat, such as grapes, pomegranates, and figs.

We would learn to lean on God when we met obstacles such as giant people and their fortified walls. We, too would be shown His signs and miracles, just as He did for them before.[10]

Let's find the good in what He's already given us, pray about the obstacles in our way, and believe that He is directing our steps toward our own Promised Land. He will give us the victory!

Seeking God's Will

After God struck down the ten-tribe leaders, the Israelites realized their grave mistake and became sorrowful for what they had done. They said, "Let's go, we realize we have sinned, but now we are ready to enter the land the Lord has promised us."[11]

"But Moses said, 'Why are you now disobeying the Lord's orders to return to the wilderness: It won't work. Do not go into the land now. The Lord is not with you.'"[12]

But they didn't listen; instead, they went, were attacked, and killed. The others wandered in the desert for forty years.

Like the Israelites, God gives us choices. We can do our own thing and go our way if we choose. Just as the Israelites had Moses, we have Jesus as our mediator. We can come to Him with our requests and directions for our lives. He who hears us is faithful to show us His will.

The Message Version of Philippians 4:6-7 says, "Don't fret or worry. Instead of worrying, pray. Let petitions and praises shape your worries into prayers, letting God know your concerns. Before you know it, a sense of God's wholeness, everything coming together for good, will come and settle you down. It's wonderful what happens when Christ displaces worry at the center of your life."

When we keep seeking His direction in prayer and do not give up, He will show us the way.

Life to the Full

Many of us can be like the Israelites in our relationship with Jesus. At first, He called us out of our slavery to sin, and we followed, just like the Israelites did from their slavery in Egypt. But their reward was the promised land, and our reward is being in a right relationship with the Father and serving Him with the plans He has for each of us.

According to the Brittanica Dictionary, the "promised land" is defined as:

- The land that was given to Abraham and his descendants according to the promise God made in the Bible, or
- The promised land: a happy place or condition that someone wants to reach: a place where dreams or hopes can come true. They came to America searching for the promised land. [13]

Many of us received the initial benefits when we became Christians: in a right relationship with God, freedom from sin and guilt, and deliverance from spiritual death. But have not yet followed Him into the land He wants to give us now: a place of peace, satisfaction, and fulfillment as His people, not just when we get to heaven.

When we don't reach the "promised land" in our lifetime, we become discontented in our friendships, marriages, and workplaces. We become restless, unsatisfied, and wanting.

Each one of us can have that abundant life right here and now if we choose. Some of us are exactly where we are supposed to be, but we struggle with being grateful for what God has given us. For others, we must put in the faith work to do what He is calling us to even when we can't see where we are going.

My Confidence is in the Lord

Let's end the chapter with a Scripture from Jeremiah 17:5-8

This is what the Lord says:
'Cursed is the one who trusts in man, who draws strength from mere flesh and
whose heart turns away from the Lord.

That person will be like a bush in the wastelands; they will not see prosperity when it comes. They will dwell in the parched places of the desert, in a salt land where no one lives.

But blessed is the one who trusts in the Lord, whose confidence is in him. They will be like a tree planted by the water that sends out its roots by the stream. It does not fear when heat comes; its leaves are always green. It has no worries in a year of drought and never fails to bear fruit.

Like the Israelites, we may not understand what God is doing in our lives. Our situation may look hopeless. We may get scared, anxious, and doubtful that He will see us through a difficult time. But we must put our trust in Him and not in our circumstances or what the unfaithful in the land say. He will give us victory when we put our trust and confidence in Him. So, keep going and do not give way to fear.

Therefore, I will listen, watch, and wait, and continue writing my book on Thursdays. Although I don't have much time to focus on marketing my book, it's not the right time to leave my workplace now. But I trust He will guide me through the process when I'm ready.

Questions

1. How did Moses know that God was giving the Israelites the promised land? How do we know when God is calling us forward to pursue the goals and dreams He's put on our hearts? How does God use our faith and perseverance to fulfil the plans He has for us?

_____

_____

_____

_____

2. What obstacles did the Israelites encounter when they were sent to assess the Promised Land? What did Joshua and Caleb do to overcome them? What are the obstacles keeping you from achieving your goals and what will you do to overcome them?

_____

_____

_____

_____

3. Write down the plans you believe God is calling you to. Recommit to them and list the next steps you need to take. Visualize them happening or visit a person who is living a dream close to what yours looks like. Believe that God is making "a way in the wilderness" and "rivers in the desert" for it to happen just as He did when He parted the Red Sea.[14]

_____

_____

_____

_____

Reflection

We all need faithful friends in our lives. Joshua and Caleb found strength in each other's faith and trusted in God's help in the face of opposition. What faithful friend can you look to for support when troubles come your way? How can your faith help someone else overcome their obstacles?

_____

_____

_____

_____

God's Promise

"Let us not become weary in doing good, for at the proper time we will reap a harvest if we do not give up."

Galatians 6:9

We all get weary when too much time, or too many obstacles come between us and what God is calling us to do. When this happens, it's good to step back, reevaluate and remember His promises. Then we can recommit to our goals with faith and action.

Take some time now to list the things you need to do to get back on track and begin believing again.

_____

_____

_____

_____

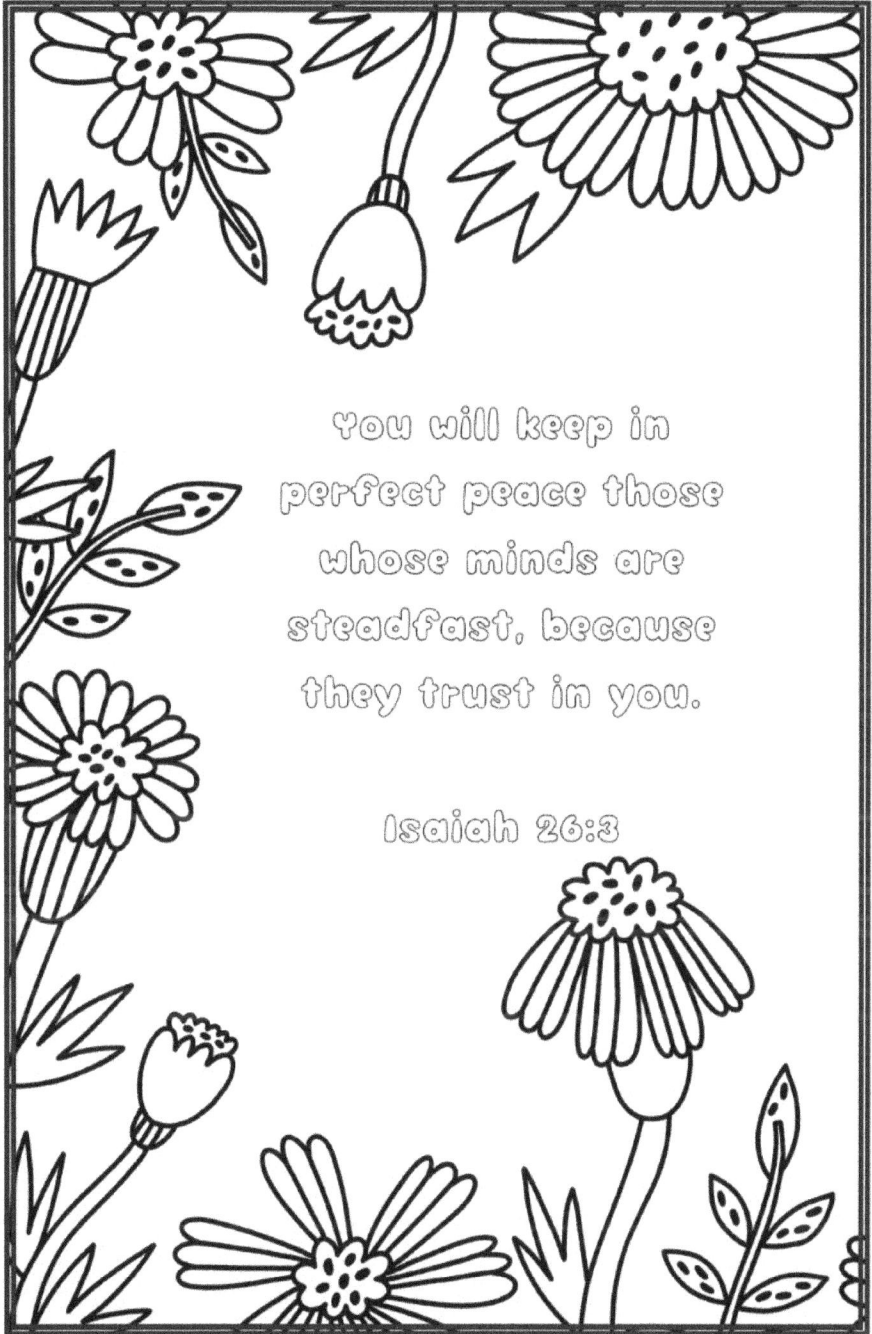

You will keep in perfect peace those whose minds are steadfast, because they trust in you.

Isaiah 26:3

Chapter Nine

Overcoming

"To him who overcomes I will grant to sit with Me on My throne, as I also overcame and sat down with My Father on His throne."

Revelation 3:21 (NKJV)

I came home from the breakfast award ceremony for my son in the wrong frame of mind. I couldn't shake my mood as I sat in my dining room, reflecting on the event that just took place. I was partly irritated and partly discouraged. I thought about the conversation I had with one of the ladies who sat at the same table as us. She and her husband had just retired and were looking forward to moving to Cape Cod. I was happy for them, but I knew my husband wasn't planning on leaving his job anytime soon. In fact, he told me he planned on working ten more years before he would retire. We needed the health benefits, and besides, he loves his job.

As I continued to feel sorry for myself, my phone pinged with a message from a friend. In her text, she said she was praying for me about a different issue and asked if there was a time someday, we could catch up. Immediately I phoned her, and she picked up.

I told her about my struggle with work, how I wanted to write my book, about the lady at the ceremony, and my husband's plans to work for ten more years. In her wisdom, she related to what I was going through, told me to trust God and take it one day at a time. *Good advice.*

Friendships

I don't know what I would do without godly friendships in my life. These are the people who know me well, listen to me, and offer me words of encouragement when needed. They help me to overcome my struggles.

Without Godly friendships, I'd hate to see where my negative thinking would have taken me. Talking through my worries with a trusted friend helped me see my situation with a new perspective. I realized I wasn't trusting God with my future. So, I told myself, *Trust in the Lord with all your heart, and lean not on your own understanding. In all your ways, acknowledge him, and he will make your paths straight.*[1] And once again, I was surrendered and at peace.

Good friendships are a gift from God. We need at least a few good friends who know us, and we can go to in our time of need. If I go too long without connecting with a good friend or two, I begin to feel like I'm all alone in my own bubble, even when others are around.

I have another friend to whom I relate on a different level. She is a spiritual counselor. With her, I do most of the talking. I decided to see her weekly because a good friend suggested it might be helpful. I was stuck in wrong thinking patterns and needed professional help to change them. She, too, is a gift from God.

During our first couple of Zoom meetings, my counselor had me take a temperament test developed from one of the oldest based "personality type" systems in the world. The outcome would reveal my natural born disposition. (See Appendix 2)

I followed the directions as they were written and answered each question quickly with my gut response. To my dismay, the results showed I was a "melancholic," but my counselor said I was acting like a "sanguine." I must admit, she was spot on. It's no wonder I had stress. I behaved in a way contrary to my natural temperament because somewhere deep down I felt the social butterfly was a more desirable personality type to be. During this realization, I thought, no wonder I like alone time and limit my social activities. *What other characteristics don't belong to me that I try to take on as my own?*

The four temperament types, sanguine, choleric, melancholic, and phlegmatic were first developed by the Greek physician Aelius Galenus and are still used today.[2]

Medical practitioners and Waldorf Schools worldwide have used this information to successfully treat their patients, and better understand and connect with their students.

In the Waldorf School, "the theory is that a child who feels held and seen in their temperament can more easily move beyond it and into more balance as they grow up. For example, a melancholic child who feels the 'weight of the world' and takes things in very deeply should not be told to 'get over it,' or, 'it's not that bad,' or 'just let it go and smile.' Instead, they respond best to a loving adult who acknowledges their pain or misery and does not try to fix it."[3]

When my counselor gave me the results of my temperament type, at first, I rejected it. I didn't want to be my type even though it fit me completely. But then she told me the upside to my temperament, that melancholics were geniuses. I thought, *well, now that doesn't sound too bad.* The point is, I wanted to be someone I was not. I wanted to be sanguine, the gregarious, fun-loving one who knew what was going on with everyone in the room. But God determined me to be, and all the other parts of His body, just as He wanted them to be.[4]

So, instead, I accept the way God made me and embrace myself. And in doing so, I continue to reap the benefits of living true to who I am. Now, I'm more selective with what I put down on my social calendar. I have limited energy, so I must choose my activities to ensure I have peace at the end of the day. When I carefully plan my days as I seek the Lord's guidance, I find myself more at ease while still being effective. I'm grateful for friends who were willing to tell me the truth.

Jesus said, "There is no greater love than to lay down one's life for one's friends."[5] We may never lay down our lives in physical death for our friends, but when we put aside our desires, wants, and needs to help someone else, this is where we can begin. Jesus is our G.O.A.T.[6] friend, to borrow an acronym from my sixteen-year-old son. He died for you and me so we might lay down our lives to help our friends and be free to live our authentic selves in His image.

Mind Change

Paul tells the Christians in Rome, "Don't copy the behavior and customs of this world but let God transform you into a new person by changing the way you think. Then you will know what God wants you to do and how good, pleasing, and perfect His will is."[7]

Before Paul's encounter with Jesus, he was an angry and violent man. He persecuted Christians, bound them, and even put them to death.[8] After his encounter with Jesus and his baptism, he was a different person and preached that Jesus was the Son of God.[9]

When the newly converted Paul went to Athens, he still had feelings of anger upon seeing all the idols that were there, but he no longer reacted with violence and force as before. Instead, he reasoned with the people in the marketplace, showed self-control and plainly told them the good news of Jesus's resurrection.[10]

In Colossae, Paul prayed for an open door to proclaim God's message clearly to the people as he should.[11] He no longer acted on his impulses persecuting the people there but relied on God for help to extend them grace, instead. He was a changed man.

Who are you Patterning?

When trying to overcome worldly patterns, it is a challenge to live in this world and not imitate its ways. Psychologists have studied the way people tend to mirror, or mimic those whom we like, even without realizing it. According to Django web developer Michael Yarbrough:

> People used mirroring as a universal signal. Humankind had to learn and invent many things to survive and evolve, including socially accepted behavior. There were stronger, smarter, and more honored individuals in human society. These were the ones with a higher social status. All the others had to develop certain behavioral patterns to show their respect and honor to the strongest. For

example, if such an honored man wore a handkerchief as a decorative accessory, the rest of the group would consider it to be trendy and an absolute must for them to wear, too.[12]

Other people rebel against socially acceptable behaviors and try not to conform. These groups still imitate one another, but in their non-compliance.

According to history.com, the hippie movement of the 1960s came about because a group of people felt that they did not fit in with the stereotypical standards of society for the time.

> The vast majority of hippies were young, white, middle-class men and women who felt alienated from mainstream middle-class society and resented the pressure to conform to the "normal" standards of appearance, employment, or lifestyle. By wearing their hair long and growing beards (for the men), taking drugs, and exploring spirituality outside of the confines of the Judeo-Christian tradition, hippies sought to find more meaning in life—or at least have a good time.[13]

For many people, this way of living resulted in promiscuity, teen pregnancies, divorces, and sexually transmitted diseases. Not such a good time in the end. Today's non-conformity may look different, but as we know, "there's nothing new under the sun,"[14] the author of Ecclesiastes proclaims.

We must be careful not to conform to the pattern of the world by evaluating ourselves by our jobs, incomes, and community statuses. Instead, we identify ourselves as God's dearly loved children, made in the image of God.

Gender Stereotyping

In addition, we must be careful not to follow the world's ways in assigning specific attributes to men and women. The Office of the High Commissioner for Human Rights in the United Nations defines gender stereotyping as follows:

A gender stereotype is a generalized view or preconception about attributes or characteristics or the roles that are or ought to be possessed by or performed by women and men. A gender stereotype is harmful when it limits women's and men's capacity to develop their personal abilities, pursue their professional careers, or make life choices.

The Qualities of Jesus

If we look at the gender of Jesus, He was male, yet He showed us many stereotypical female characteristics during His ministry on Earth. For example, He was vulnerable with His close friends and shared His emotions with them in The Garden of Gethsemane.[15] He wept over the lost Jeruselum[16] and cared about people. It says, "When Jesus landed and saw a large crowd, he had compassion on them because they were like sheep without a shepherd. So, he began teaching them many things."[17] By the world's standards, these acts would be stereotyped as "feminine" qualities. However, He also exhibited the stereotypical male qualities of truth-telling, fearlessness, bravery, and the like. Hopefully, we can all learn to imitate the qualities of Jesus with the freedom to express all of His characteristics.

Jesus was a carpenter's son. In those days, His occupation was considered lower on the pecking order than a peasant farmer. I imagine He wasn't rich, yet He was never in want, either. He didn't concern Himself with money. He knew the hold it had on people; how deceitful it was. He seemed to stay far away from it. When He began His ministry, He accepted support from His followers, Mary, Joanna, Suzanna, and many others, as they had means.[18]

He taught those who held fancy parties not to look down on others, nor to think so highly of themselves. Instead, He said when they gave a banquet, they were to invite the poor, the crippled, the lame, the blind; then they would be blessed. He promised them, "although they could not repay you, you will be repaid at the resurrection of the righteous."[19]

He did not need the best seat at the synagogue, nor to be greeted respectfully in the marketplace. He wasn't always liked, nor accepted by people, especially by the religious community. In fact, they often were insulted when He spoke the truth to them. How was He able to do this? He knew who He was and why He was there. He had His Father's marching orders, and His approval, and that was enough.

Jesus loved everyone, even the religious leaders. When He was invited to have a meal with them, Jesus waited for the opportunity to rebuke them in their arrogance, and errors, in the hope they might turn from their pious ways. He taught them what was most important, calling them foolish, greedy, and wicked not just to get their attention, but also because it was true! He cared more about saving souls, then saving face. Certainly, this is not the same one-dimensional Jesus we see in photographs, who is gentle, meek, and gathers lambs:

> When Jesus had finished speaking, a Pharisee invited him to eat with him, so he went in and reclined at the table. But the Pharisee was surprised when he noticed that Jesus did not wash before the meal.
> Then the Lord said to him, "Now then, you Pharisees clean the outside of the cup and dish, but inside you are full of greed and wickedness. You foolish people! Did not the one who made the outside make the inside also? But now, as for what is inside you— be generous to the poor, and everything will be clean for you."
> "Woe to you Pharisees, because you give God a tenth of your mint, rue, and all other kinds of garden herbs, but you neglect justice and the love of God. You should have practiced the latter without leaving the former undone."
> "Woe to you Pharisees, because you love the most important seats in the synagogues and respectful greetings in the marketplaces."
> "Woe to you, because you are like unmarked graves, which people walk over without knowing it."
> One of the experts in the law answered him, "Teacher when you say these things, you insult us also."
> Jesus replied, "And you experts in the law, woe to you, because you load people down with burdens they can hardly carry, and you yourselves will not lift one finger to help them."[20]

Yes, Jesus insulted people by pointing out their evil deeds. In doing so, He hoped they might change their ways and keep their souls from death. As it is written in Psalm 141:5 "Let a righteous man strike me-it is a kindness; let him rebuke me-it is oil for my head; let my head not refuse it. Yet my prayer is continually against their evil deeds."

He was closest to the repentant undesirables and disreputables who followed Him. He was loyal to them despite their faults and betrayals. He desired to be with these people even when they messed up at times.

God created all of us in His image, both male and female. There are no stereotypes when it comes to loving people, serving them, speaking the truth in love, and forgiving others. There are no stereotypes in giving and receiving God's grace. We no longer hold onto what the world values, nor in the ways it judges us, but we remember we are accepted by our loving Father in Heaven because of what Jesus did for us. No longer do we wish to follow the ways of the world, but our desire is to imitate His ways for all our lifetime.

Training to be Godly

My son works out regularly with his high school football team. They train three days per week during the off season and six days per week in the regular season. They do this to build their bodies and skill sets to be ready for game day. It's hard work.

When he gets home from practice, he's tired and worn out. But because of his great effort, he's earned his desired position on the varsity team.

In the same way, training ourselves to be godly takes work. It takes training to overcome persistent sin and align wrong thought patterns to the Truth.

I have a bulletin board in my kitchen where I pin index cards of key verses that help me overcome my wrong thinking. I write them in my favorite translations for more power. I highly recommend reading a passage in a translation other than what you're used to. Hearing God's Truth in a new way may help you to gain victory over a persistent struggle. Below are my current go-to scriptures for this season in life:

- When I'm feeling insecure about myself: "So God created mankind in his own image, in the image of God he created them; male and female he created them."[21]
- When I can't decide what to do: "I have the right to do anything," you say—but not everything is beneficial. "I have the right to do

anything—but not everything is constructive."[22]

- When I'm tempted to worry about what others may think of me: "My victory and honor come from God alone. He is my refuge, a rock where no enemy can reach me."[23]

- When I feel guilty or accused: "So now there is no condemnation for those who belong to Christ Jesus."[24]

- When I don't feel I deserve happiness: "I know that there is nothing better for people than to be happy and to do good while they live."[25]

- When my enemy does me wrong or hurts my feelings: "But love your enemies, do good to them, and lend to them without expecting to get anything back. Then your reward will be great, and you will be children of the Most High because he is kind to the ungrateful and wicked."[26]

The Peace of Christ

The peace of the world is quite different from the soul peace Jesus intended for us to have. We may vacation on a sunny island and call it peace, but God had more in store for us than bodily rest. Jesus said, "I have told you these things so that in Me you may have peace." [27]

The kind of peace Jesus offers is the soul tranquility that those of us in Christ have. Since He overcame the world, and even death on a cross, we are now in a right relationship with Him. There is no more hostility between us. We can trust God entirely with no fear of ill-treatment from Him. He richly gives us our earthly portions and gives us contentment in them. He promises to always be with us, and never forsake us. He gives us satisfaction and joy. Our cups overflow. We are free. Free from accusation and condemnation, to live out the earthly and heavenly plans He has in store for us. *Oh, how deeply He longs for all His creation to receive this rest of the soul.*

Questions

1. Do you have two or three good friends that know you well and with whom you feel comfortable talking to about your struggles? If not, pray now for God to reveal them to you and make a way to bring them into your life.

_____

_____

_____

_____

2. Training is hard work. What false thinking patterns do you have that don't line up with God's Truth? What scriptures will you choose to help train your mind with His thoughts? Find the translation that holds the most power to demolish the strongholds in your heart.

_____

_____

_____

_____

3. A gender stereotype is a generalized view or preconception about attributes, characteristics or the roles thought to be possessed or performed by a certain gender group. In what other groups of people did Jesus break stereotypes? How do you think this motivated them for change?

_____

_____

_____

_____

Reflection

In the Western world, we may imitate the diet culture around us with its body image norms. Social media tells us to diet, nip, tuck, and buy the latest fashions to be accepted and beautiful. But God tells us that our "beauty should not come from outward adornments, such as braided hair, the wearing of gold jewelry and fine clothes. Instead, it should be that of (our) inner self, the unfading beauty of a gentle and quiet spirit, which is of great worth in God's sight."[28]

What cultural norms have you fallen victim to that are not biblical or no longer serve you? How will you find the support to help you overcome them and find peace and freedom in God's Truth?

_____
_____
_____
_____

God's Promise

"As He approached Jerusalem and saw the city, He wept over it and said, "If you, even you, had only known on this day what would bring you peace—but now it is hidden from your eyes."

Luke 19:41-42

Jesus wanted to bring peace to the lost people of Jerusalem. What was the promise of peace He was offering them?

_____
_____
_____
_____

Chapter Nine - Crossword Puzzle
Directions: Use the Clues Below to Complete the Crossword Puzzle that Contain the Words in 1 Peter 5:8

"Be self-controlled and alert. Your enemy the devil prowls around like a roaring lion looking for someone to devour."

Across

1. Eat hungrily or quickly

4. The chief evil spirit, satan

5. A person who is actively opposed to or hostile to someone or something.

6. Moves around restlessly and stealthily, especially in search of or as if in search of prey

7. Quick notice of any unusual and potentially dangerous or difficult circumstances, vigilant

Down

2. Making or uttering a loud, deep, or harsh prolonged sound

3. Restraint exercised over one's own impulses, emotions, or desires

Chapter Nine - Crossword Puzzle

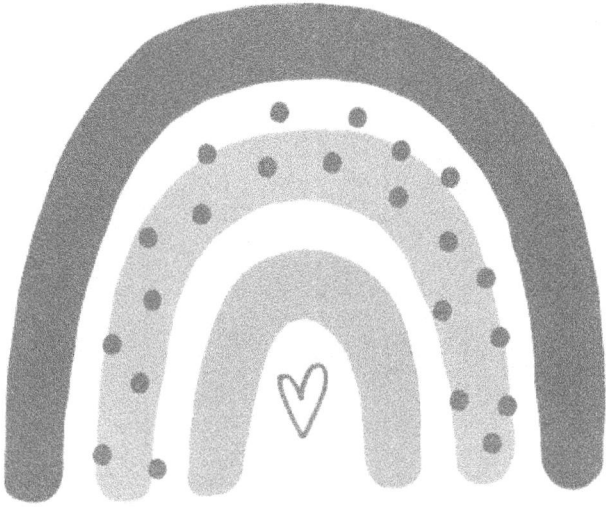

Part 4

Purposeful Life

I end this book in reflection about things still unresolved in my life:

My son left to go back to his home state of California. I drove him to the airport and saw him off. I still had unsettled feelings in my heart that only time and surrender to God would help. This situation required more prayer, and release of control on my part while asking for wisdom and strength to speak the truth in love the next time we saw each other.

I don't know whether I will stay at my teaching job. I will see what September holds. Through this process, I've learned that wherever I go, my sinful nature follows me. Therefore, I must change my ways, or my situation is bound to repeat itself. I also pray to be on the same page as God, wherever His work takes me as He knows what's best.

We are in the middle of downsizing our home. We sold our house but haven't found a new one yet. Without a home to set up my office space, my book and business venture is still just a twinkle in my eye. In addition, it's a seller's market and houses are in short supply. Often there are bidding wars with homeowners asking for final and best offers from their buyers. If we don't find a home soon, we'll have to rent an apartment.

But I trust God. He is amazing and faithful.

When I awoke in my bed this morning, a scripture came to my mind. I wanted to study it out so I got up, made my coffee, and sat at my quiet time spot on the bench in the vestibule in the house which in one week's time would be inhabited by another family. Even so, today it was a sanctuary, and my soul was at rest.

I turned to the Book of Habakkuk and read until my faith grew greater than the sun in full day. *Yes, God was still at work through all the unknowns in my life.*

Here's a portion of it:

Though the fig tree does not bud and there are no grapes on the vines, and the olive crop fails, and the fields produce no food, though there are no sheep in the pen and no cattle in the stalls, yet I will rejoice in the Lord, I will be joyful in God my Savior.

The Sovereign Lord is my strength; He makes my feet like the feet of a deer; He enables me to go on the heights.[1]

We have great faith when we can praise God in our times of uncertainty. Not only do we please God, but we may save our hearers, and ourselves.

Thank you, God, for the plans you have for us today, tomorrow, and forevermore.

Thought Questions

1. Do you think the Christian life is one with no troubles?

2. What is the difference between believing His promises and claiming them?

3. What does life to the full mean to you?

Chapter Ten

Life to the Full

"The thief comes only to steal and kill and destroy; I have come that they may have life and have it to the full."

John 10:10

The results of my Enneagram test showed I was an adaptive type four. According to Marilyn Vancil's book Self to Lose, Self to Find, "This type of person 'overdoes being special.' They avoid being ordinary or blending in. They believe no one else could ever grasp the depths of their internal world and fear being misunderstood (by people).

Yes, that's me. Although others may not be able to meet me in the depths of my soul, I knew God would.

And I added this to my list of learning new things about myself.

I don't believe the Enneagram, or any temperament test is the end-all-be-all method for identifying our character traits. But they can be helpful tools for self-awareness of our strengths and weaknesses as we look to God to mature us in all the fruits of the Spirit: love, joy, peace, patience, kindness, goodness, faithfulness, gentleness, and self-control.

In order to grow, we must be in community with others. Having a few good spiritual-minded friends in our lives can help us see ourselves as we mature into Christ. The Book of Proverbs says, "A man's heart is deep waters, but a man of understanding will draw it out."[1]

Oftentimes when we talk to others, we simply need to listen to our own faulty thinking and see that it doesn't line up with Truth or reason. Then we can change it and continue on the right path. Friends who listen and ask the right questions can help us discern what's in our hearts. They are gifts from God.

I wrote this book in part to understand what it meant to have life to the full. I wanted to receive all that God had to offer me in a relationship with Him through the blood of Christ. Then I wanted to share it with others so that we might be mutually encouraged, faithful until the end.

When I completed my first manuscript, I held a 5-week book club with some of my friends and gave them each a copy to read. Over the course of ten weeks, they came over my house (or Zoomed) and we went over the questions in the back of each chapter. We shared our triumphs, and tribulations. We connected with each other, but most of all, we remembered who we are, and all that we have in Christ.

Claiming the Promises

Beloved, I've included some of God's promises that pertained to the themes in this book: the promises of peace, power, freedom, faith, hope, love, and eternity with God forever. Remember who you are.

Promises of Peace

- "Do not be anxious about anything, but in every situation, by prayer and petition, with thanksgiving, present your requests to God. And the peace of God, which transcends all understanding, will guard your hearts and your minds in Christ Jesus." (Philippians 4:7)
- "You will keep in perfect peace those whose minds are steadfast because they trust in You." (Isaiah 26:3)
- "I have told you these things, so that in Me you may have peace. In this world you will have trouble. But take heart! I have overcome the world." (John 16:33)

Promises of Power

- "But those who hope in the Lord will renew their strength. They will soar on wings like eagles; they will run and not grow weary; they will walk and not be faint." (Isaiah 40:31)
- "But He said to me, "My grace is sufficient for you, for My power is made perfect in weakness." Therefore, I will boast all the more gladly about my weaknesses, so that Christ's power may rest on me." (2 Corinthians 12:9)

Promises of Freedom

- "When we follow Jesus' teachings, we are His true followers. Then we will experience the Truth, and It will free us." (John 8:31-32)
- "Christ has set us free to live a free life. So, take your stand! Never again let anyone put a harness of slavery on you." (Galatians 5:1 MSG)

Promises of Faithfulness

- "To the faithful, You show Yourself faithful." (Psalm 18:25)
- "Faith shows the reality of what we hope for; it is the evidence of things we cannot see." (Hebrews 11:1)
- "Jesus replied, "Truly I tell you, if you have faith and do not doubt, not only can you do what was done to the fig tree, but also you can say to this mountain, 'Go, throw yourself into the sea,' and it will be done. If you believe, you will receive whatever you ask for in prayer." (Matthew 21:21-23)

Promises of Good Works

- "For we are God's handiwork, created in Christ Jesus to do good works, which God prepared in advance for us to do." (Ephesians 2:10)
- "Being confident of this, that He who began a good work in you will carry it on to completion until the day of Christ Jesus." (Philippians 1:6)

Promises of Companionship

- "And Jesus came and said to them, 'All authority in heaven and on earth has been given to me. Go therefore and make disciples of all nations, baptizing them in the name of the Father and of the Son and of the Holy Spirit, and teaching them to obey everything that I have commanded you. And remember, I am with you always, to the end of the age." (Mathew 28:18-20)
- "Never will I leave you; never will I forsake you." (Deuteronomy 31:8)

Promises of Love

- "This is how everyone will know that you are my disciples when you love each other." (John 13:35)
- "We love because He first loved us." (1 John 4:19)
- "Greater love has no one than this, that someone lay down his life for his friends." (John 15:13)

Promises of Eternity

- "Whoever hears My Word and believes Him who sent Me has eternal life. He does not come into judgment but has passed from death to life!" (John 5:24)
- "For God so loved the world that He gave His One and Only Son, that whoever believes in Him shall not perish but have eternal life." (John 3:16)
- "I give them eternal life, and they shall never perish; no one will snatch them out of My hand. My Father, who has given them to Me, is greater than all; no one can snatch them out of My Father's hand. I and the Father are One." (John 10:28-30)

Our Very Great Reward

Finally, in Hebrews 11:1, it says, "To have faith is to be sure of the things we hope for, to be certain of the things we cannot see." And Hebrews 11:6 says, "No one can please God without faith, for whoever comes to God must have faith that God exists and that he rewards those who seek him."

Without faith, we cannot please God, nor have a relationship with Him. He is the source of our peace, and power, and the keeper of all His promises Our faith is precious to Him, worth more than riches in His sight. With it, we have found our very great reward, and maybe some other amazing surprises along the way.

Because of Jesus, it is all ours for the taking, if we claim it as our own.

Questions

1. In the first part of John 10:10 b, Jesus says, "I have come that they may have life..." What does life mean to you?

_____

_____

_____

_____

2. Which of the promises listed at the end of this chapter did you resonate with most? Why?

_____

_____

_____

_____

3. According to Hebrew 11:1, and 11:6, what does it mean to have faith? What is our reward for coming to Him with faith that He exists?

_____

_____

_____

_____

Reflection

The Enneagram is a personality test that can be a helpful tool for self-awareness and identifying our strengths and weaknesses. Find a free Enneagram quiz on-line and take it for yourself.

What are some of the traits that line up most with your personality? (See Appendix 3) How might this information help you to grow more Christ-like?

_____

_____

_____

_____

God's Promise

"But you are a chosen people, a royal priesthood, a holy nation, God's special possession, that you may declare the praises of him who called you out of darkness."

1 Peter 2:9

When we became Christians, we became God's people, his special possessions, who receive His mercy. Knowing this, we can declare His praises to others, and live free to be all He made us to be. What does this promise mean to you?

_____

_____

_____

_____

I have said these things to you, that in me you may have peace. In the world you will have tribulation. But take heart: I have overcome the world.

John 16:33

Epilogue

One Question

"If you could ask Jesus one question, what would it be?" Our small group leader asked us after service on Sunday. We all took turns sharing our responses.

"How do I consistently love people and not choke them?" asked one sister in the group.

"Am I going to get to heaven? Will I get in?" asked another who was recently restored.

"Do you like sweet or savory?" said another as we all chuckled at the idea that Jesus may have had a preference.

All of us finished with our responses except the leader of the group. So, I asked him, "What would you ask Jesus?"

He replied, "Why? Why do we have to go through all this? Why do we need to live out the lives you gave us?"

The sister who recently came back to church answered his question easily. "He wanted someone to love." And we all said, "Aww."

But isn't it true?

He wanted companionship. He wanted us with Him.

God desired to love us, to be with us. Each of us was a thought in His mind before we came to be. He wanted us to belong to Him and each other. He accepted, loved, and approved of us. He wanted to satisfy us with good things and have us share in His glory.

He equipped us, then gave us the work of our hands to do while we're here.

For many, accepting God's love is difficult. It can be foreign, hard to recognize. We're not used to this lay-down-your-life kind of love. We may run from it. We may hide in fear of what we may discover about ourselves because of it. But no matter, He did it. He laid down His life for us.

It may be challenging to obey His Words, seek His direction, trust, and submit to His plans, and follow Him; but the alternative is, we grieve the Holy Spirit and ignore our soul's longings for the life He calls us to live.

If we are honest, the false, manufactured self with its insecurities, striving and frequent discontentment will never satisfy us overall compared to the peace God wants us to have by accepting ourselves, as we are, as God's creations, warts, and all!

When we put our hope in the wrong things, such as status, success, beauty, or achievement, we choose inferior replacements for true riches. Yet He longs for us to take our rightful place in His Kingdom so that we might claim all His promises and live peaceful and powerful lives, shining bright and giving Him the glory.

Let's be the people who live out our God-given designs and who perform the work He calls us to do. Let's continue to seek Him first, holding onto the Truth of His Words, throwing off the lies as we worship Him only, and accept our reconciled lives with God because of what Jesus did on the cross. When we know we are loved by God, we can love others in the same way as we spur one another on toward love and good deeds. When we do, we will live full, contented lives now and for eternity. Are you up for the challenge? And the chosen ones say, "Yes, please!"

Believe.

Rewrite your top 5 areas of life where your faith
was small and rate them again on a scale of
1-10.* Reflect on your ratings on the lines below
and thank God for caring for you as He does.

*10 means I'm not worried at all, you're faithful God
is working and 1 is extremely worried/you lack faith,
God is not working in this area of my life.

Appendix 1

Types of Learning Styles
What type of learner are you?

Visual **LEARNS BY SEEING**	Auditory **LEARNS BY HEARING**
• Charts, Graphs • Graphic Organizers • Lesson outlines • Picture aids • Power Points	• Read-aloud • Listening centers • Verbal instructions • Discussions • Repeat to a friend
Read & Write **LEARNS BY READING & WRITING** • Books & texts • Dictionaries • Notetaking	Kinesthetic **LEARNS BY DOING** • Incorporate body movement • Tactile - touch, feel • Hands-on

Appendix 2

The Temperaments

Temperament	Strengths	Weaknesses
Choleric Extroverted and arrogant Tough and domineering Leadership and independence	-Strive for independence -Strong determination -Honesty -Tough and confident	-Lack of tolerance -Competitive -Haughty pride
Sanguine Social and Expressive Talkative and playful Emotional and volatile	-Friendliness -Easy to forgive	-Haughty pride -Obsession for attention -Forgetfulness or lack of intimate relationship -Poor organization.
Melancholy Perfectionistic Less friendly Extremely logical	-Careful planning -Search for reason and logic -Faithfulness in friendship	-Easily offended -Self-guilt -Self-condemnation at the slightest mistake -Pessimism -Lack of tolerance
Phlegmatic Calm and introverted Passionate and great listeners Indecisive and peaceful	-Faithfulness in friendship -Non-judgmental -Great listening ability -Ability to distribute glory and efficiently dissipate defeat	-Indecisiveness -Lack of self-confidence

Appendix 3

Overview of the Nine Enneagrams*

Enneagram Number	Title	Characteristics
1	The Reformer	Rational, Idealistic
2	The Helper	Caring, Interpersonal
3	The Achiever	Success-Oriented, Pragmatic
4	The Individualist	Sensitive, Withdrawn
5	The Investigator	Intense, Cerebral
6	The Loyalist	Committed, Security-Oriented
7	The Enthusiast	Busy, Fun-Loving
8	The Challenger	Powerful, Dominating, Protective
9	The Peacemaker	Easygoing, Self-Effacing

*The Enneagram is a tool used to gain self-knowledge

Answers to Puzzles

Chapter One - Verse Find
Proverbs 3:5-6

```
T  E  S  D  L  T  O  W  U  A  W  R  S  V  B
R  K  B  H  L  B  C  O  M  F  I  K  U  S  G
G  C  P  O  Q  G  O  T  R  U  S  T  V  B  G
X  G  E  F  U  H  D  W  C  N  U  O  W  U  I
M  I  R  L  P  G  X  D  I  D  B  T  D  O  T
U  C  L  E  F  U  D  P  Z  E  M  B  O  U  X
W  A  Y  S  J  R  X  F  O  R  I  S  S  E  K
L  T  D  O  G  Z  Q  H  M  S  T  T  X  Y  X
D  D  Q  N  U  L  A  E  A  T  R  R  Y  R  H
K  G  W  L  O  R  D  U  K  A  H  A  X  N  T
G  O  P  A  E  T  X  U  E  N  B  I  Y  D  I
A  Z  Y  F  P  A  T  H  S  D  E  G  W  S  A
D  L  R  H  X  Q  N  T  G  I  X  H  K  U  D
Q  M  F  S  G  J  R  X  A  N  C  T  B  F  M
D  A  F  A  L  D  O  O  U  G  D  M  W  M  J
```

Chapter Two - Crossword Puzzle
Romans 5:3-5

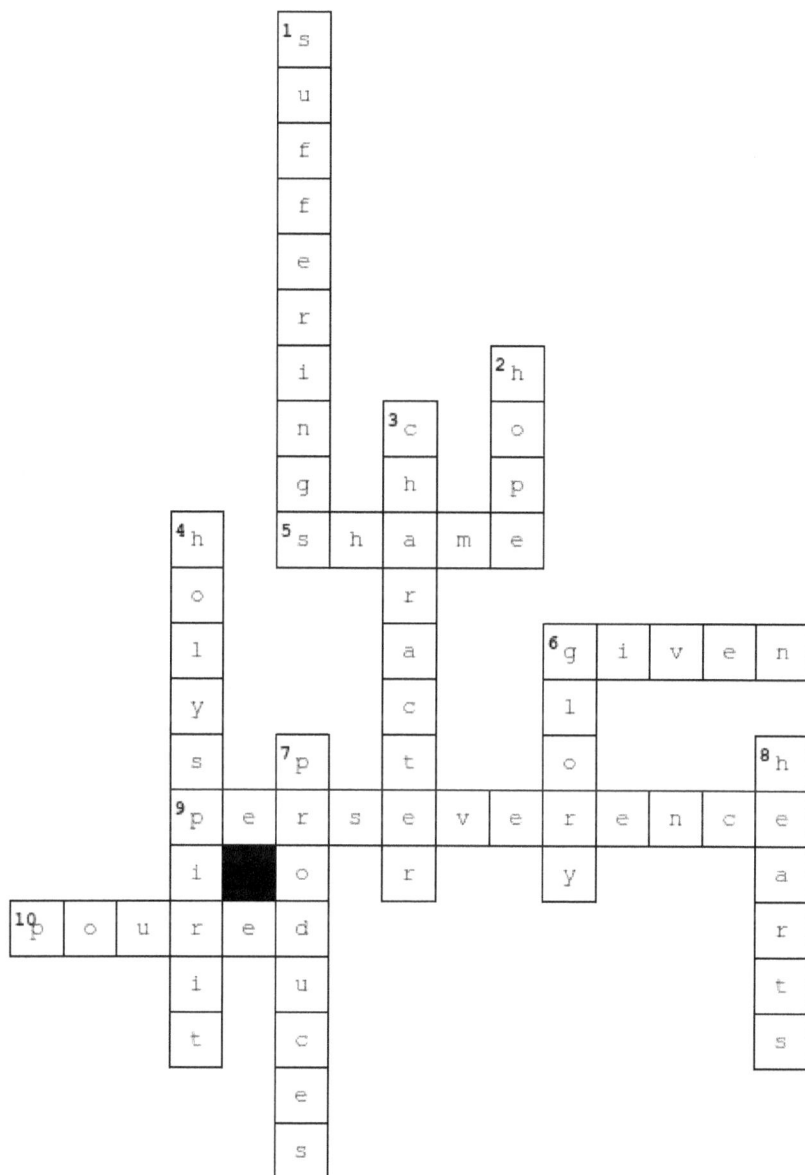

Across:
5. shame
6. given
9. perseverence
10. poured

Down:
1. suffering
2. hop
3. character
4. holys
7. produces
8. hearts

Chapter Three - Verse Find
Ecclesiastes 3:1, 3:6b (MSG)

```
M  U  G  L  V  H  M  T  U  A  N  K  F  S  X
R  A  V  Q  K  P  V  E  L  Q  Z  I  N  U  Z
R  P  I  T  M  Y  R  V  V  H  S  P  Y  C  S
B  B  F  E  W  Z  L  E  M  E  O  U  P  C  O
C  H  R  U  N  D  E  R  I  A  R  L  P  M  M
U  R  T  D  L  F  T  Y  Q  V  S  Y  D  T  G
Y  A  C  T  I  V  I  T  Y  E  K  W  O  S  O
U  G  L  D  I  C  M  H  H  N  F  C  N  T  R
F  H  I  C  C  L  E  I  I  S  A  H  X  T  Z
F  H  R  G  V  E  O  N  F  A  J  S  X  C  E
J  D  S  K  O  L  A  G  X  L  Y  N  M  X  V
I  L  G  R  S  E  A  S  O  N  H  W  M  L  X
B  L  B  J  Y  T  H  E  R  E  I  S  H  M  K
F  Y  S  I  P  Q  S  X  W  N  H  U  E  I  A
V  U  U  S  L  A  Q  S  M  C  H  I  F  B  P
```

Chapter Four - Verse Find
2 Corinthians 12:10

```
M  T  Y  D  R  A  N  V  X  D  P  Z  W  C  E
W  W  W  E  A  K  N  E  S  S  E  S  E  W  V
R  F  R  H  H  R  W  I  Q  Z  R  T  A  J  R
G  Q  L  I  E  A  J  I  Z  I  S  R  K  K  I
I  A  U  E  Z  N  R  B  N  W  E  O  M  F  E
I  E  Q  R  D  U  I  D  P  S  C  N  A  C  S
Q  P  K  H  E  I  J  E  S  T  U  G  H  H  E
M  V  Q  D  V  N  O  L  W  H  T  L  B  R  N
G  Q  V  J  D  I  U  I  T  E  I  Z  T  I  C
V  C  S  J  G  R  S  G  X  N  O  P  S  S  P
W  P  T  R  A  J  S  H  B  U  N  D  S  T  P
Y  H  C  T  C  V  G  T  H  Z  S  J  O  S  J
E  J  J  C  G  W  D  V  Q  D  L  Q  R  W  D
D  I  F  F  I  C  U  L  T  I  E  S  J  T  P
T  Y  V  N  X  V  Q  P  E  W  M  Q  T  G  H
```

Chapter Six - Crossword Puzzle
Philippians 4:5-7

Chapter Seven - Verse Find
Isaiah 43:1

```
V  O  S  J  Q  M  I  K  U  V  X  Y  R  S  Z
Z  G  S  G  Q  S  W  Y  G  M  J  H  E  U  K
V  F  K  N  K  H  D  U  A  O  H  T  D  Z  Q
S  X  E  M  V  E  T  J  C  E  Y  S  E  N  T
X  H  G  A  I  I  R  X  O  P  L  J  E  O  L
V  F  F  D  Y  N  A  M  E  W  T  F  M  F  J
H  N  D  B  B  T  E  R  H  B  L  U  E  W  N
G  N  U  O  Z  C  B  F  E  A  R  B  D  D  M
V  H  S  X  D  W  A  A  Y  Y  V  W  T  N  S
X  Z  M  F  Q  S  U  M  M  O  N  E  D  V  V
O  Z  O  R  X  P  S  L  P  U  U  N  O  T  Z
T  R  E  C  B  Y  W  L  G  K  D  Y  W  A  L
Y  C  Z  O  P  U  B  T  M  G  F  O  M  G  P
V  H  L  L  K  A  C  C  J  P  B  N  G  V  M
X  Y  N  O  Q  O  Y  B  D  Q  N  G  H  L  Y
```

Chapter Nine - Crossword Puzzle
1 Peter 5:8

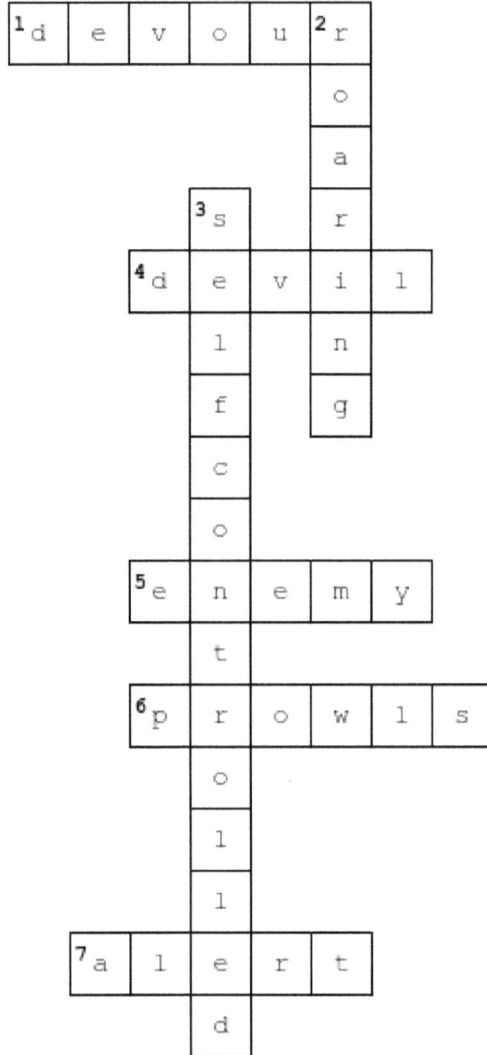

```
¹d  e  v  o  u  ²r
               o
               a
      ³s       r
   ⁴d  e  v  i  l
      l        n
      f        g
      c
      o
   ⁵e  n  e  m  y
      t
   ⁶p  r  o  w  l  s
      o
      l
      l
⁷a  l  e  r  t
      d
```

References

Introduction
1. Psalm 8:4-8, NLT.
2. See Romans 8:28.
3. Isaiah 30:21, ISV.
4. Psalm 23:3, NLT.
5. Ephesians 2:10.
6. See Isaiah 55:8-9.
7. Jeremiah 29:11.

Chapter 1
1. https://www.youtube.com/watch?v=TFkR7CjVd9U.
2. Proverbs 3:5-6.
3. The Best lyrics © Mike Chapman Publishing Ent., Knighty Knight Music, Mike Chapman Publishing Enterprises Inc., Music Corp. Of America, Inc.
4. See John 1:12, John 3:16, Psalm 139:13-14, Romans 8:28, Matthew 25:14, Psalm 103:5 John 15:16, Matthew 7:7a, Ephesians 2:10.
5. See Psalm 139:2, 13, Jeremiah 1:5, Genesis 1:27, Luke 11:13.
6. See Deuteronomy 31:6-8, Luke 12:12, Proverbs 17:27-28.
7. See 1 Corinthians 13:4, Matthew 6:8, 1 Peter 2:9, 2 Corinthians 1:3-7.
8. See Romans 8:1, Romans 6:18, 1 John 1:9, 2 Corinthians 5:17, Romans 6:6, Ephesians 1:7.
9. See John 15:15, Psalm 103:5, Proverbs 3:5-6.
10. See 1 John 2:2, Luke 2:11, John 10:28, Romans 8:31-39, Joshua 1:9b.
11. See Colossians 3:1-4, Philippians 3:20, 1 Corinthians 12:18, Psalm 23:5-6, 2 Peter 1:3.
12. See Acts 2:46-47, Romans 1:6, Romans 15:7, 1 Corinthians 12:26.
13. https://www.lyrics.com/lyric/16578339/Barry+White/You%27re+the+First%2C+The+Last%2C+My+Everything.
14. https://genius.com/Bryan-adams-everything-i-do-i-do-it-for-you-lyrics.
15. All of Me lyrics © BMG Rights Management, Warner Chappell Music, Inc.

Chapter 2

1. See John 16:33.
2. See 2 Corinthians 5:7.
3. See Galatians 6:9.
4. See Luke 2:46.
5. See Luke 5:16.
6. See Matthew 4:1.
7. See Philippians 2:6-8.
8. See Matthew 26:40-45.
9. See John 8:6-8, Matthew 15:1-9.
10. See Luke 7:11-15.
11. See Luke 14:13-14.
12. Ibid.
13. See Matthew 15:24.
14. See John 5:1-14.
15. See Luke 4:29.
16. See Matthew 5:21-24.
17. See Matthew 27:12.
18. See 1 Peter 2:23.

Chapter 3

1. https://www.songfacts.com/facts/michael-sembello/maniac.
2. John Mark Comer. (2019). The Ruthless Elimination of Hurry. Waterbrook.
3.https://www.nps.gov/cham/learn/nature/upload/Hummingbirds-of-Chamizal_english.pdf.
4. See 1 Timothy 6:3-4.
5. Ecclesiastes 3:1-8.
6. See Mark 11:24.
7. See John 14:27.

Chapter 4

1. See John 16:33.
2 See 1 Peter 5:6.
3.https://www.lyrics.com/lyric/22966527/Lincoln+Brewster/Everlasting+God.

4. See Matthew 5:1-5.
5. See Hebrews 4:16.
6. https://www.cslewisinstitute.org/resources/reflections-december-2008/.
7.https://positivepsychology.com/humility.
8. Ibid.
9. James 1:19.
10. https://positivepsychology.com/humility.
11. https://www.desiringgod.org/articles/humble-yourself-like-god.
12. Ibid.
13. 1 Peter 5:6.
14. Philippians 2:6-8.
15. Philippians 2:10.
16. See Ephesians 5:21.
17. See 2 Timothy 1:7.
18. See Hebrews 10:39.
19. See Psalm 32:9.
20. https://positivepsychology.com/humility.
21. Luke 2:49.
22. Psalm 16:6.
23. See Luke 14:10b.

Chapter 5
1. See 1 Timothy 4:7.
2. See Romans 3:23.
3. See Ephesians 2:8-9.
4. See Psalm 62:7.
5. See Psalm 33:9.
6. See 2 Peter 1:21.
7. See Hebrews 4:12.
8. See Ephesians 5:11.
9. See Rom 15:13.
10. See Jer 29:11.
11. See Hebrews 4:13.
12. See 1 Corinthians 3:6-7.
13. See Isaiah 55:11.

14. BIOY@ copyright Alpha International.
15. See James 1:22.
16. See Matthew 28:20.
17. See John 14:9.
18. See John 6:63.
19. See John 6:68.
20. Proverbs 18:21.
21. James 3:9.
22. Mark 13:11.
23. Mark 11:24.
24. Matthew 12:34.
25. Matthew 9:4.
26. Ephesians 4:27.
27. See 1 Corinthians 9:20-22.
28. See 1 Corinthians 7:7.
29. Colossians 4:2-4.

Chapter 6

1. Ecclesiastes 7:9.
2. https://www.glccalaska.org/retreatprep.
3. 1 John 4:16.
4. See Matthew 6:9–13.
5. See John 16:33.
6. See Ephesians 6:18.
7. See 1 Thessalonians 5:16-17.
8. See 1 Samuel 13:14.
9. Proverbs 27:17.
10. See Ephesians 4:30.
11. See John 16:13.
12. See Psalm 16:3.
13. See 1 John 4:18.
14. See Philippians 4:6-7.
15. See Colossians 4:6.
16. See Psalm 46:10.
17. See 1 Peter 5:7.
18. See Isaiah 32:17.

19. See Psalm 118:6.

Chapter 7
1. See Matthew 19:16-26.
2. See Matthew 6:24.
3. See Luke 15:10.
4. See Matthew 25:23.
5. See Isaiah 1:17.
6. John 15:4-8 .
7. See Galatians 5:22-23a.
8. See Isaiah 26:3.
9. Skye Jethani, *With: Reimagining the Way you Relate to God* (Thomas Nelson 2011), 117-119.
10. See Deuteronomy 31:8.
11. See John 19:30.
12. See Matthew 27:51.

Chapter 8
1. See Numbers 13:1-19.
2. Numbers 13:27-28.
3. Numbers 13:30.
4. Numbers 13:31-33.
5. See Numbers 14:1-4.
6. Numbers 14:5-9.
7. Numbers 14:10-12.
8. See Numbers 14:36-38.
9. Numbers 14:39-40.
10. See Numbers 14:11.
11. See Numbers 14:40.
12. See Numbers 14:42.
13. https://www.britannica.com/dictionary/Promised-Land.
14. See Isaiah 43:19.

Chapter 9
1. Proverbs 3:5-6.
2. https://www.dailywonderhomelearning.com/blog/

the-four-temperaments.

3. Ibid.

4. See 1 Corinthians 12:11.

5. John 15:13.

6. G.O.A.T. acronym, Greatest of All Time.

7. Romans 12:2.

8. See Acts 26:9-11.

9. See Acts 9:18-22.

10. See Acts 17:16-34.

11. Colossians 4:3-4.

12. https://medium.com/the-mission/the-surprising-truth-about-why-we-tend-to-imitate-others.

13. Ibid.

14. Ecclesiastes 1:9.

15. See Matthew 26:36-46.

16. See Luke 19:41-42.

17. See Mark 6:34.

18. See Luke 8:3.

19. See Luke 14:12-14.

20. Luke 11:37-46.

21. Genesis 1:27.

22. 1 Corinthians 6:12.

23. Psalm 62:7.

24. Romans 8:1.

25. Ecclesiastes 3:12.

26. Luke 6:35.

27. John 16:33.

28. 1 Peter 3:3-4.

Part IV

1. Habakkuk 3:17-19.

Chapter 10

1. Proverbs 20:5.

Appendix 1
www.tejedastots.com/Learning styles.

Appendix 2
https://www.knowseeker.com/lifestyle/the-four-temperaments-strength-weakness-ultimate-temperament/.

Appendix 3
https://www.chicagocounseling.com/blog/enneagram-overview.

About the Author

MaryAnn Kasper became a Christian in 1995 and met her husband, Joey, at church while serving together in the singles ministry. She earned a Master's Degree in Special Education while teaching in the NJ Public Schools for ten years. They live in NJ with their pug named Molly, and are almost empty nesters to three grown sons, Zach, Harry, and Hunter. You can see what she's up to at maryannkasper.com

Journal Pages

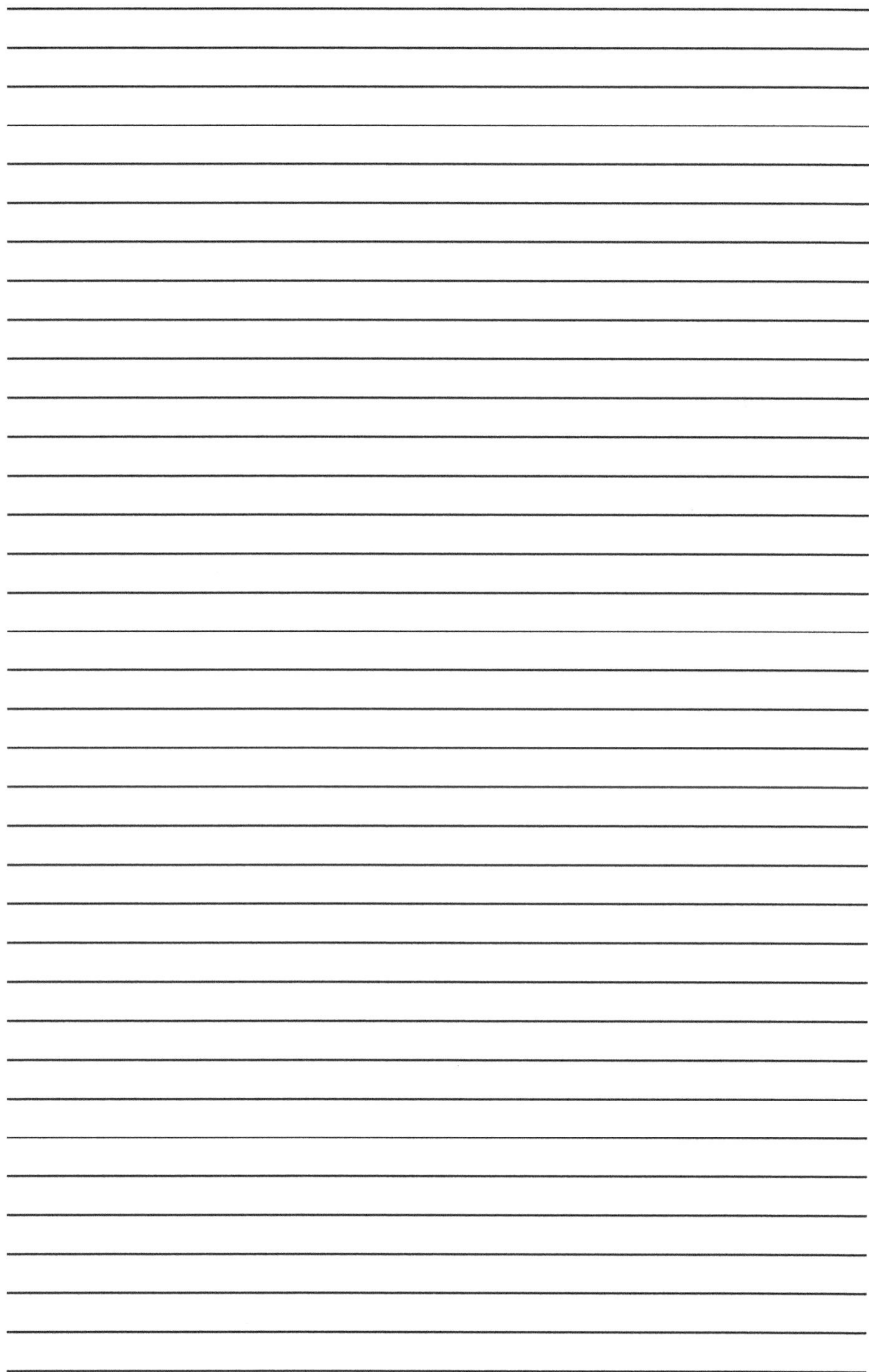

www.ingramcontent.com/pod-product-compliance
Lightning Source LLC
Chambersburg PA
CBHW071217090426
42736CB00014B/2867